ANSWERS
TO QUESTIONS
YOU *always*
WANTED TO
ASK

DAVID WEST

SIMON & SCHUSTER

LONDON • SYDNEY • NEW YORK • TOKYO • SINGAPORE • TORONTO

For Jamie and Oliver

Designed and created by
N.W. Books
28 Percy St
London W1P 9FF

Designs and illustrations by
David West Children's Book Design
Text by John Clark, David West,
Charles De Vere, Bill Hemsley

First published in 1991 by
Simon & Schuster Young Books

Simon & Schuster Young Books
Wolsey House
Wolsey Road
Hemel Hempstead HP2 4SS

Printed and bound in Belgium
by Proost International Book
Production

British Library Cataloguing in
Publication Data

West, David
  Answers to questions you always
    wanted to ask
  I. Title
  507.24
  ISBN 0 7500 0858 X
  ISBN 0 7500 0859 8

INTRODUCTION

Humans have always asked questions. Even prehistoric man must have wondered why the Sun went down at night and how fire gave off heat. It's only when we start to question the things we take for granted that we can learn about ourselves, our world and the worlds beyond us. And it's our inquisitive nature that has dragged us from the rock-throwing ape of 10 million years ago to the computer-tapping technician of today.

CONTENTS

OUR WORLD

Why do we see lightning before we hear thunder? Lightning is a flash of light made when electricity jumps from a cloud. Thunder is the sound made by the lightning. But light travels 100,000 times faster than sound. The speed of light is 300,000 kilometres a second, whereas sound travels at only 345 metres a second. So we see lightning before we hear thunder. The time that passes between a lightning flash and the crash of thunder tells you how far away the storm is – each 3 seconds represents a kilometre distance.

ANSWERS TO QUESTIONS YOU *always* WANTED TO ASK

Why doesn't the Sun go out?

The Sun will eventually burn out. But this will not happen for another ten billion years. The Sun is a huge ball of gas, mostly hydrogen, and it produces heat by converting this hydrogen into helium. On earth, we produce the same kind of energy in the devastating explosion of a hydrogen bomb. As the Sun uses up its hydrogen, it will begin to swell and turn into a red giant. In old age, it will collapse into a small, heavy form of star called a white dwarf. Eventually this will stop shining and it will become a black dwarf.

OUR SUN

What is inside the Sun?

The Sun is made of about 75 percent hydrogen and 25 percent helium. The core at the centre of the Sun is at a temperature of 15,000,000°C, and is made of highly compressed helium atoms. In the radiative layer hydrogen fuses to make helium, creating the Sun's energy. In the convective layer gases churn around at about 1,100,000°C. The surface of the Sun, called the Photosphere, is the visible part of the Sun and has a temperature of about 5,500°C. Above the surface is the Chromosphere where violent flares and prominences can be sometimes seen.

What are sunspots?

Sunspots are dark areas on the Sun's surface created by a build-up of magnetic forces. These areas look darker because they are cooler than the rest of the surface.

Chromosphere

Photosphere

Convective zone

Radiative layer

Prominence

Size of our Earth compared to the Sun

Core

Sunspots

What is a white dwarf?

Many red giants become white dwarfs. As the stars cool further the gas cloud is blown away, leaving a white-hot embers at the core. At this stage they are called white dwarfs. As they cool down they may become black dwarfs.

Red giant

Black dwarf

White dwarf

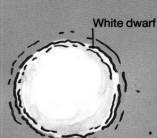

What is a red giant?

When certain stars run out of fuel they begin to cool down and start to collapse, causing increased nuclear reactions in the centre of the star. The outer gases of the star expand, and the energy from the centre starts new nuclear reactions in these gases, too. The star continues to expand and when viewed through a telescope looks redder than other stars. Red giants can have diameters as much as 100 times that of the Sun.

What is a black hole?

Black holes form when certain types of stars reach the end of their lives. A star collapses and becomes enormously dense. The gravity of such a star would be so great that if an astronaut was being sucked into it and was trying to send a message by light we would not see it. This is because even light cannot escape!

What causes earthquakes?

The surface layer of the Earth (the mantle) is made up of about 20 plates. These plates are grinding very slowly past each other. As they move, they put great pressure on the rock at their edges. Sometimes they stick and the pressure builds up. Suddenly they snap apart, which causes shock waves to travel through the Earth. These shock waves are an earthquake. The energy in the shock waves of a big earthquake can be about the same as the energy of exploding 200 million tonnes of TNT.

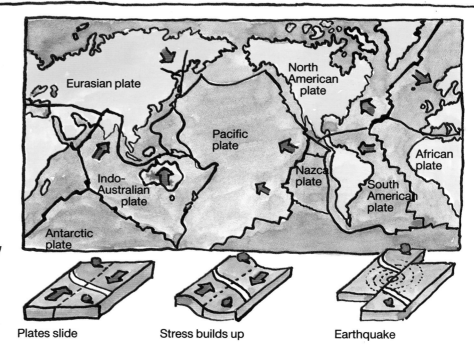

Plates slide   Stress builds up   Earthquake

Where does lava come from?

The Earth is made up of layers. The cool, hard surface layer is called the crust. Beneath this is a layer called the mantle, which is mostly made of solid, but very hot, rock. Below the mantle is the core. The temperature of the core near the mantle is as much as 2,200°C. The heat of the core can melt rocks in the mantle. As the rock melts, it produces a lot of gas. The molten rock (called magma) is quite light and moves upwards, melting a path through the mantle. It gathers in chambers, under great pressure because of the gas. If there is a weak part of the crust, the magma melts a path to the surface. When it reaches the surface, it is known as lava and flows out from erupting volcanoes.

Where do mountains come from?

The Earth's crust is always on the move in various directions. These areas of crust are known as plates. When two plates collide they wrinkle and buckle forming mountain ranges (fold mountains). Sometimes molten magma forces its way to the surface to form ridges and mountains.

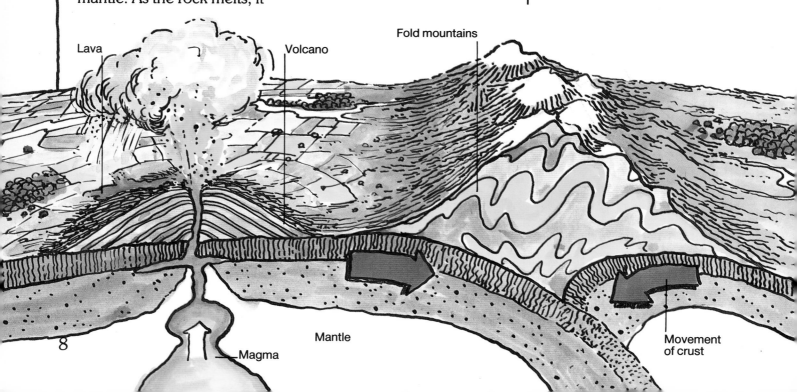

Lava   Volcano   Fold mountains

Mantle

Magma

Movement of crust

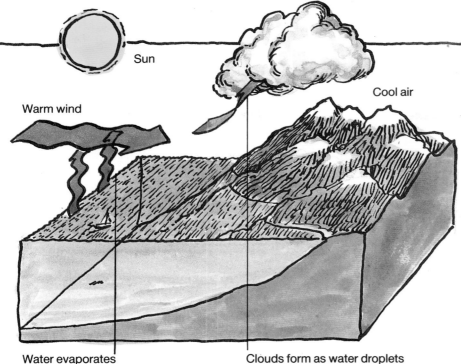

Sun

Warm wind

Cool air

Water evaporates

Clouds form as water droplets collect together as they cool

Where do clouds come from?

The air always contains some invisible water vapour. The heat of the Sun causes water to evaporate from the surfaces of rivers, lakes and seas. If for any reason the water vapour in the air is cooled, perhaps because winds force it to rise over mountains, the vapour condenses into tiny droplets of water. When these water droplets collect together they form clouds. When you breathe out on a frosty day, the water vapour in your breath condenses into similar droplets and you make your own clouds.

What makes the winds blow?

When the Sun shines on the land and the oceans, it warms them up. But it does not heat them evenly – some places become hotter than others. Air over the hot places expands and rises. When it does so, air from cooler places rushes in to take its place. It is these air movements that we call the wind.

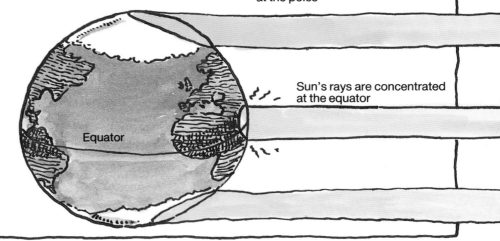

Hot air rises

Cold air rushes in

WIND

Why is it hotter at the Equator than at the poles?

The temperature in any particular region of the world depends mainly on how much of the Sun's warming rays it receives. And this depends, in turn, on the angle that the surface of the Earth makes with the rays. The Sun is so far away that its rays are parallel when they arrive at the Earth. Near the Equator, the Sun is directly overhead at mid-day and its rays shine straight down on the surface. But near the poles, the Sun never climbs far above the horizon

and its rays reach the surface at an angle. This means that the rays are much more spread out over the surface.

Sun's rays are spread out at the poles

Sun's rays are concentrated at the equator

Equator

How old is the Earth?

The Earth was formed, along with the rest of the Solar System, about 4,500 million years ago. The first life forms probably appeared about 3,500-4,000 years ago.

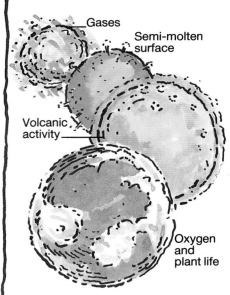

Gases
Semi-molten surface
Volcanic activity
Oxygen and plant life

What is the Earth's crust made of?

The Earth's crust, which forms the land and the ocean floors, is made of rock. Most rocks are what chemists call silicates, that is, compounds of silicon and oxygen. These are often combined with some aluminium. The most common elements in the crust are oxygen (47% by weight), silicon (28%) and aluminium (8%). There is also 5% iron, 3.5% calcium, and smaller amounts of other elements.

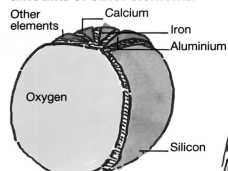

Other elements
Calcium
Iron
Aluminium
Oxygen
Silicon

What is at the centre of the Earth?

The centre of the Earth is known as the core. It is divided into two parts: the outer core and the inner core. The outer core starts about 2,900 kilometres below the surface. It is made of molten iron, nickel and a small amount of some other elements. Its temperature is between 2,000°C and 5,000°C. The inner core begins about 5,000 kilometres below the surface and is about 2,800 kilometres across. The core is again made of iron and nickel, and is solid. It is under great pressure and has a temperature of about 6,000°C. Nobody is sure of any of this. The deepest hole ever drilled reached less than a sixth of one percent of the way to the centre.

Which way does a compass point at the North Pole?

At the geographic North Pole, a compass points south. This is because a compass always points towards the magnetic North Pole, which at present is not in the same place as the geographic pole – it is in the frozen Arctic Ocean off northern Canada. At that place, a compass needle swings wildly about, not knowing which way to face. But if you turned the compass on its side, the needle would point straight down to the magnetic North Pole beneath your feet.

THE EARTH

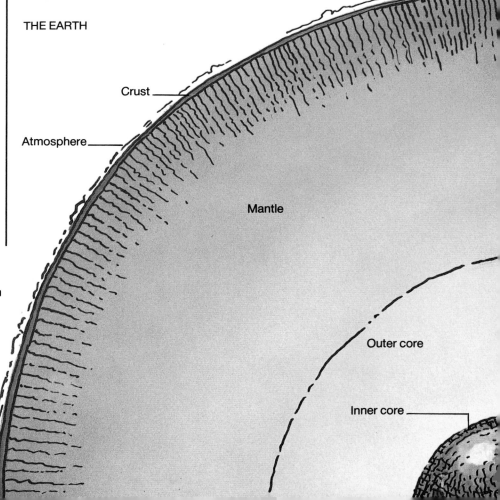

Crust
Atmosphere
Mantle
Outer core
Inner core

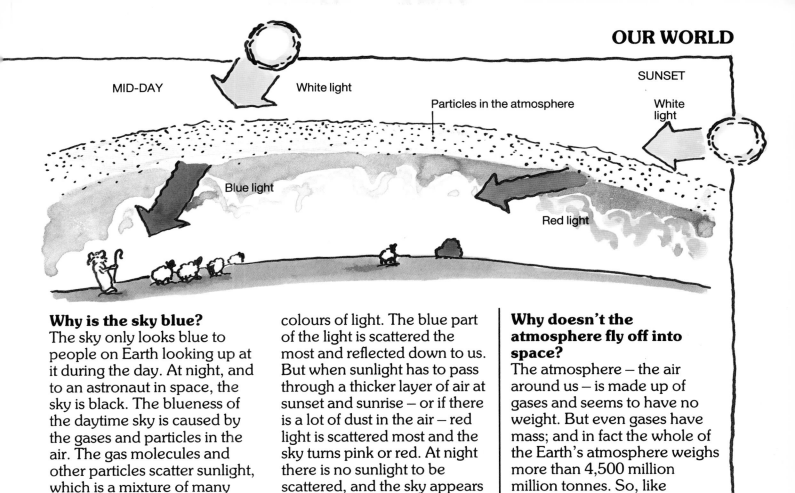

MID-DAY

White light

Particles in the atmosphere

SUNSET

White light

Blue light

Red light

Why is the sky blue?

The sky only looks blue to people on Earth looking up at it during the day. At night, and to an astronaut in space, the sky is black. The blueness of the daytime sky is caused by the gases and particles in the air. The gas molecules and other particles scatter sunlight, which is a mixture of many colours of light. The blue part of the light is scattered the most and reflected down to us. But when sunlight has to pass through a thicker layer of air at sunset and sunrise – or if there is a lot of dust in the air – red light is scattered most and the sky turns pink or red. At night there is no sunlight to be scattered, and the sky appears jet black.

Why doesn't the atmosphere fly off into space?

The atmosphere – the air around us – is made up of gases and seems to have no weight. But even gases have mass; and in fact the whole of the Earth's atmosphere weighs more than 4,500 million million tonnes. So, like everything else on Earth, it is held in place by gravity, which is the force of attraction between masses, such as between the Earth and the atmosphere. The column of air above your head and pressing on you weighs about a tonne, although you do not feel it because there is an equal pressure of air on all sides of you.

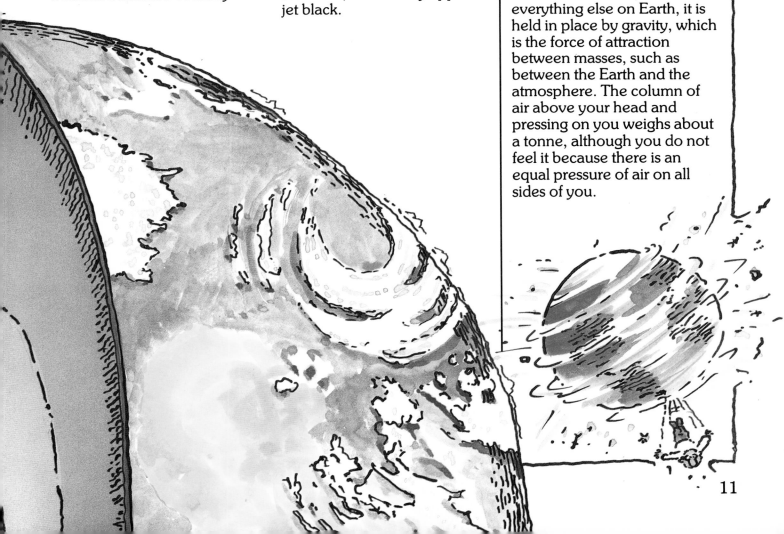

What is the greenhouse effect?

Certain gases (such as carbon dioxide and methane) in the Earth's atmosphere make the Earth and its atmosphere warm up. These gases are known as greenhouse gases. Heat rays from the Sun pass through the atmosphere and warm the ground (which in turn warms the air). These rays have a certain wavelength. When the heat is radiated out from the ground again, however, the heat rays have a different wavelength. Rays with this wavelength are blocked by greenhouse gases. This means that, if there are too many greenhouse gases in the atmosphere, the world will heat up. The term greenhouse effect comes from the fact that the glass in a greenhouse has the same effect as these gases.

THE GREENHOUSE EFFECT

Some heat is reflected back into space

Heat from Sun

Greenhouse gases

Heat from ground is reflected back causing a temperature rise

Greenhouse gases are caused by burning fossil fuels in cars, industry and power stations

Methane is a greenhouse gas

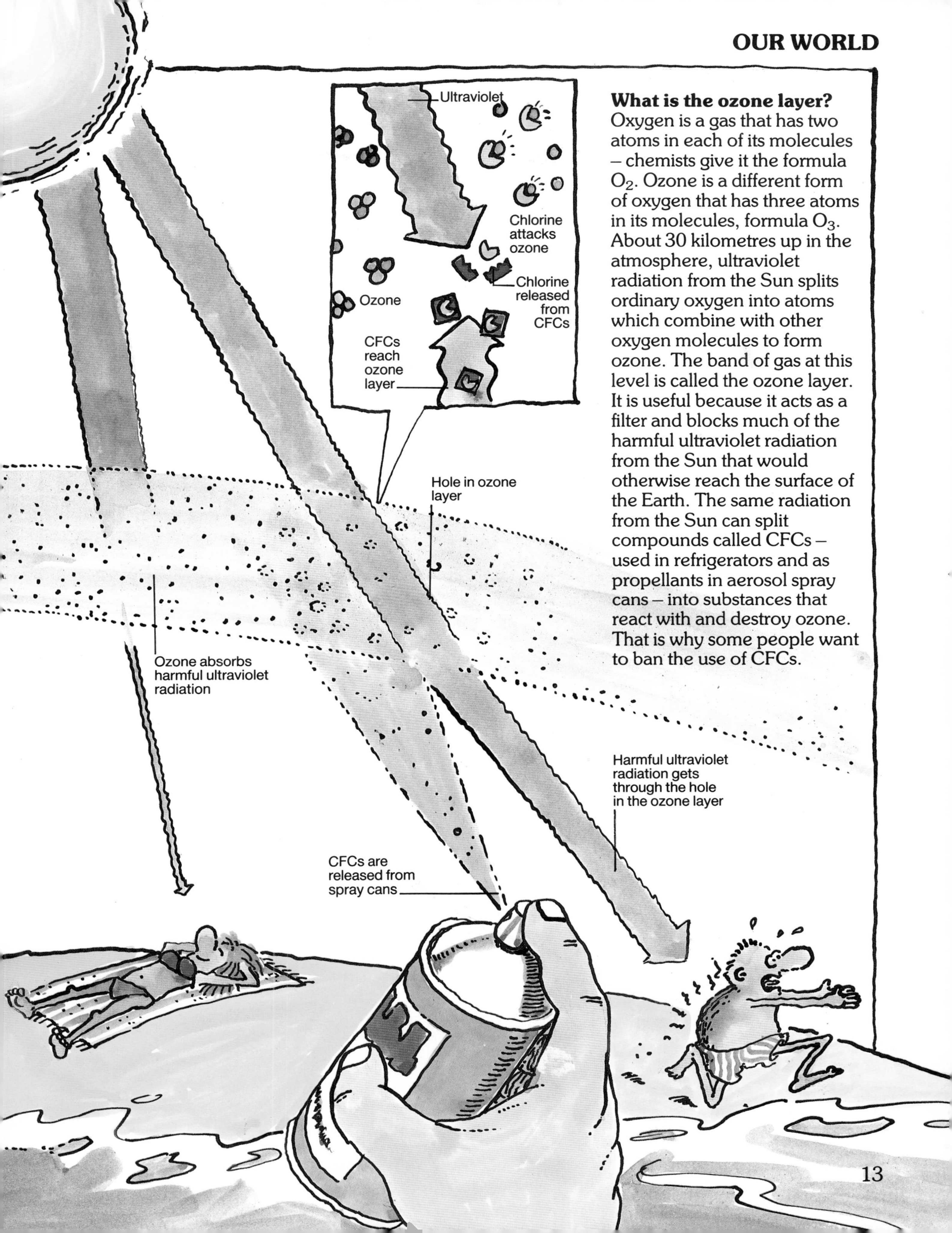

Ultraviolet

Chlorine attacks ozone

Chlorine released from CFCs

Ozone

CFCs reach ozone layer

What is the ozone layer?
Oxygen is a gas that has two atoms in each of its molecules – chemists give it the formula O_2. Ozone is a different form of oxygen that has three atoms in its molecules, formula O_3. About 30 kilometres up in the atmosphere, ultraviolet radiation from the Sun splits ordinary oxygen into atoms which combine with other oxygen molecules to form ozone. The band of gas at this level is called the ozone layer. It is useful because it acts as a filter and blocks much of the harmful ultraviolet radiation from the Sun that would otherwise reach the surface of the Earth. The same radiation from the Sun can split compounds called CFCs – used in refrigerators and as propellants in aerosol spray cans – into substances that react with and destroy ozone. That is why some people want to ban the use of CFCs.

Hole in ozone layer

Ozone absorbs harmful ultraviolet radiation

Harmful ultraviolet radiation gets through the hole in the ozone layer

CFCs are released from spray cans

Why is the sea salty?

The main salt in the sea is the same as the salt that people put on their food. Its chemical name is sodium chloride. Ordinary sea water contains about 3.5% of salts, mostly sodium chloride. This is why sea water is denser than fresh water and no good for drinking. The salt gets into the sea by being washed into it by rivers that flow from the land. The salt dissolves into rivers from earth and rocks. But scientists are puzzled by the fact that the sea is not getting steadily saltier, and has probably not changed in saltiness for millions of years.

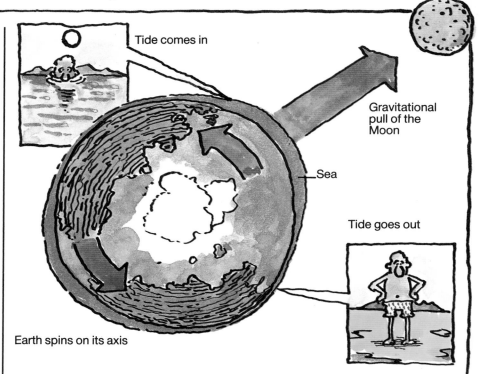

Tide comes in

Gravitational pull of the Moon

Sea

Tide goes out

Earth spins on its axis

Some seas are so salty you can float in them

Why doesn't the Earth's oxygen run out?

There are huge amounts of oxygen in the atmosphere. But if it was never replaced, it would gradually be used up by living things breathing and chemical reactions such as burning. Oxygen is replaced, however, by plants. Plants make much of their food from water, carbon dioxide and sunlight. This process, called photosynthesis, produces oxygen. A lot of oxygen is produced by land plants, but even more is produced by plant plankton in the sea.

Where does the sea go when the tide goes out?

The times of the tides are different in different parts of the world. When it is low tide at one place, it is high tide somewhere else. Tides are caused by the pull of the Moon's gravity. It causes water in the Earth's oceans to bulge towards the Moon. At the same time, there is a bulge in the oceans on the opposite side of the world as the Moon pulls the Earth away from the water. The Earth continuously rotates on its axis. About six hours after high tide in a particular place, the Earth will have made a quarter turn on its axis. This rotation will have carried the sea round so that it is no longer directly beneath the Moon and the water is not then pulled towards it. It will be low tide.

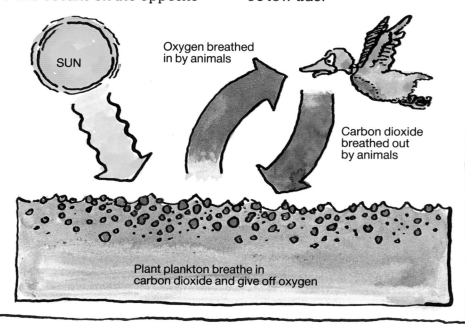

SUN

Oxygen breathed in by animals

Carbon dioxide breathed out by animals

Plant plankton breathe in carbon dioxide and give off oxygen

YOUR BODY

Why do we shiver when we're cold?
To help us get warm again. Shivering is caused by lots of rapid contractions of the muscles of the body. Using muscles generates heat – that is why you get hot after exercise – and so shivering helps to warm us up.

Why do we get goose pimples when we are cold?

All of our skin, except our lips, palms of our hands and soles of our feet, is covered with hair. The hairs may be too small to be seen easily, but nevertheless they are there. When we are cold, a tiny muscle at the end of each hair pulls it erect. The hair stands on end and the erect hairs trap air which makes an insulating layer that helps to keep the body warm. The action of the muscle also raises a small bump or goose pimple around the base of the hair.

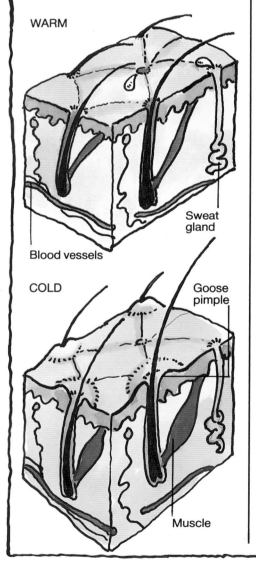

WARM

Blood vessels

Sweat gland

COLD

Goose pimple

Muscle

Sweat gland

Why do we sweat when we're hot?

To make us cooler. When you are hot after exercise or if you have a fever, tiny glands in your skin release sweat. This is a slightly salty liquid containing 99 per cent water. The water evaporates, and while doing so absorbs heat from your skin and cools you down. In hot humid places water does not evaporate. It runs off in drops, and so in these climates sweating is not as effective at cooling us down.

Why do people turn brown in the sun?

When people expose themselves to the Sun, cells in their skin produce the substance melanin. This gives them a suntan, and the darker skin is not so easily harmed by the Sun's rays. But too much sun can still cause nasty burns.

Why do we blush?

When you blush your face goes red and you can feel it getting hot. The more you think about it, the worse it gets. You go red because extra blood flows in the tiny blood vessels just under the skin. The cause is often emotional – perhaps you feel embarrassed or very shy. Also drinking alcohol or eating spicy food can make people look flushed. A hundred years ago blushing was thought to be attractive, and young women used to pinch their cheeks to make them pink.

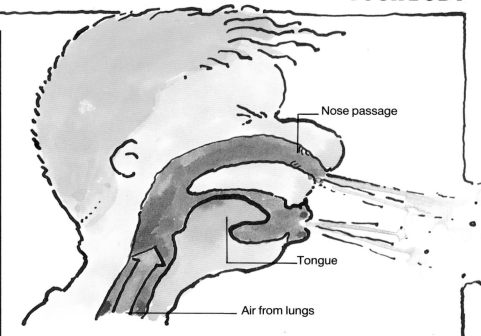

Nose passage

Tongue

Air from lungs

Why do we get a fever when we're ill?

Sometimes when you're ill, your body temperature goes up above normal (normal temperature is 37°C, or 98.6°F). This rise in temperature is called a fever, and it is triggered off by the germs that cause the illness. They release chemicals that act on the part of the brain whose job is to control temperature. This in turn produces other chemicals that make you feel cold. Your body reacts by increasing its temperature.

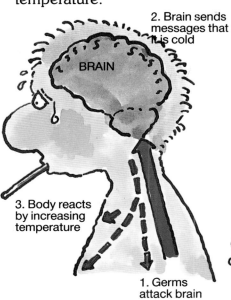

2. Brain sends messages that it is cold

BRAIN

3. Body reacts by increasing temperature

1. Germs attack brain

Why is there no cure for the common cold?

Colds are caused by one of a number of different germs. The germs are viruses, which change all the time. As with other virus diseases, there is no specific cure for a cold, only medicines to relieve the unpleasant symptoms. Even if scientists could develop a vaccine against a particular form of the cold virus, it would be of no use against the many other cold viruses.

What makes us sneeze?

Sneezing is an automatic action to remove something that is tickling inside our nose. The tickling may be caused by dust, or by the inflammation that goes with a cold or hay fever. Some people also sneeze when they look into a bright light. When we sneeze, the back of the mouth is blocked by the tongue and breath is forced violently out of the nose. Droplets of water are sprayed into the air at speeds of up to 150 km/h. Sneezing is the main way colds are spread. The world record for sneezing is held by an English girl who sneezed non-stop for more than 32 months.

There are too many types of cold viruses for vaccines to be effective

What makes us yawn?

Yawning may be brought on by tiredness, lack of sleep or fresh air, or simply boredom. It may also be caused by seeing somebody else yawn. Like sneezing, yawning is an action you cannot control. Your mouth opens wide as you first take a deep breath in, and then breathe out. Some people think yawning is a way of exercising our lungs.

What are people made of?

Like everything else in the world, people are made up of elements – the basic substances that cannot be split up into anything else. The most common elements in the human body are carbon, hydrogen, oxygen and nitrogen. Combinations of these form carbohydrates, fats, proteins and water, the substances that make up most body tissues. There are also smaller amounts of calcium and phosphorus (in bones and teeth), iron (in blood and muscles), chlorine, sodium and potassium, and tiny amounts of other elements. But most of the body (65 per cent) consists of water.

Why do we have bones?

Bones make up the framework of the body. The limb bones (in the arms and legs) and the spine provide points for muscles to attach to so that we can move. The bones of the skull, chest and pelvis protect delicate internal organs such as the brain, heart and bladder. Bones also store calcium and contain marrow, in which blood cells are made.

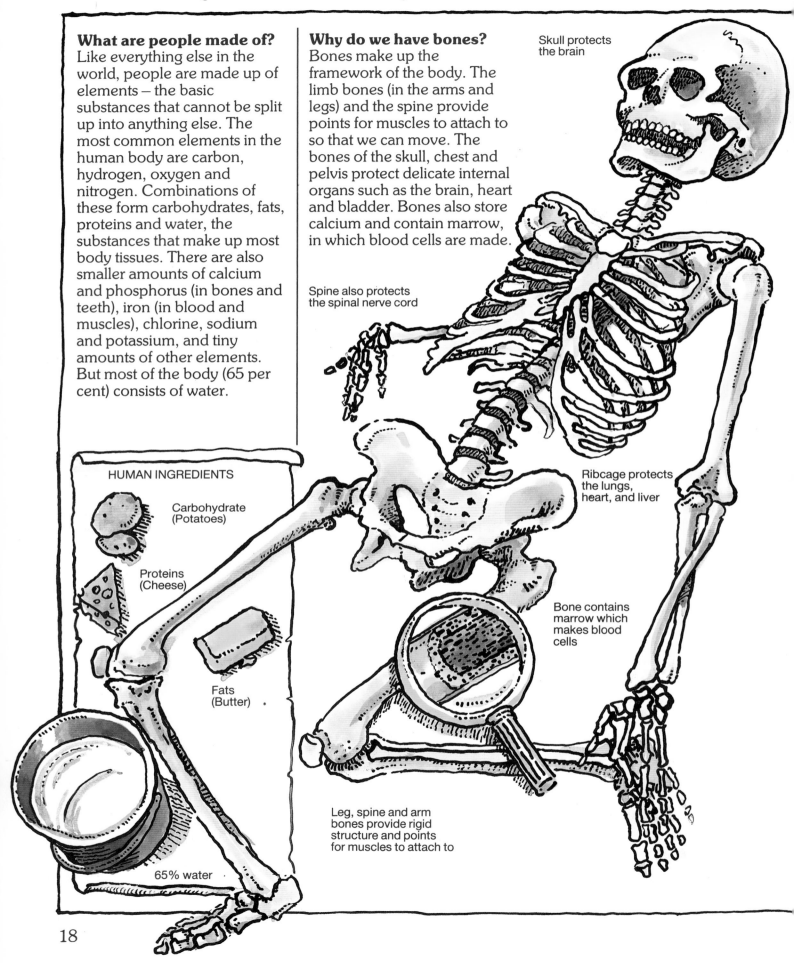

Skull protects the brain

Spine also protects the spinal nerve cord

Ribcage protects the lungs, heart, and liver

Bone contains marrow which makes blood cells

Leg, spine and arm bones provide rigid structure and points for muscles to attach to

HUMAN INGREDIENTS

Carbohydrate (Potatoes)

Proteins (Cheese)

Fats (Butter)

65% water

How many muscles are there in the body?

The human body has more than 600 muscles, which together make up more than 40 per cent of the body's weight.

The heart and digestive systems are also made of muscle tissue

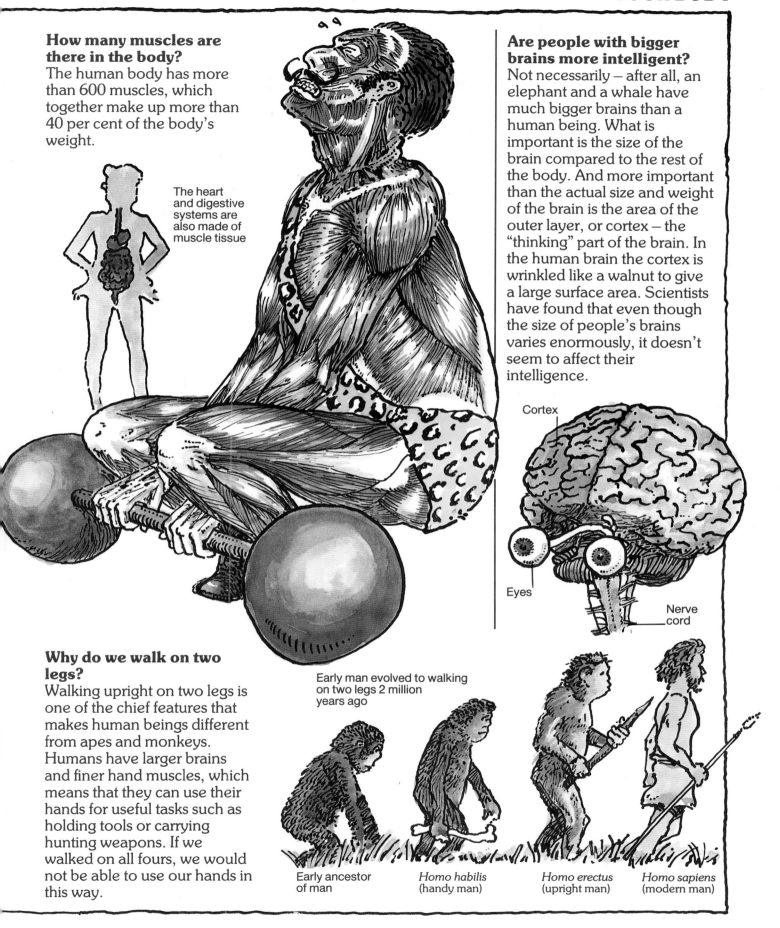

Are people with bigger brains more intelligent?

Not necessarily – after all, an elephant and a whale have much bigger brains than a human being. What is important is the size of the brain compared to the rest of the body. And more important than the actual size and weight of the brain is the area of the outer layer, or cortex – the "thinking" part of the brain. In the human brain the cortex is wrinkled like a walnut to give a large surface area. Scientists have found that even though the size of people's brains varies enormously, it doesn't seem to affect their intelligence.

Cortex

Eyes

Nerve cord

Why do we walk on two legs?

Walking upright on two legs is one of the chief features that makes human beings different from apes and monkeys. Humans have larger brains and finer hand muscles, which means that they can use their hands for useful tasks such as holding tools or carrying hunting weapons. If we walked on all fours, we would not be able to use our hands in this way.

Early man evolved to walking on two legs 2 million years ago

Early ancestor of man

Homo habilis (handy man)

Homo erectus (upright man)

Homo sapiens (modern man)

What happens to our food once we have eaten it?

To get the goodness and energy out of food, it has to be broken down into chemicals that can be absorbed into your body. This is what happens during digestion, when saliva and chewing begin to break down the food. It then passes to the stomach where it is further broken down by acid and digestive juices. After leaving the stomach, food enters the intestines where it is further attacked by digestive juices. It is then absorbed by capillaries into the blood, passing through the liver which contains thousands of enzymes which break down any poisons like alcohol, and also acts as a store of iron, vitamins and glucose. Finally food that cannot be digested is excreted as waste.

Gullet

Liver

Gall bladder

Stomach

Pancreas

How much food does the stomach hold?

An adult's stomach holds about 0.9 litres of food, although it can stretch and hold more after a particularly large meal.

Why do we get hiccups?

Most people get hiccups after eating too fast, swallowing very hot or very cold food, or drinking fizzy drinks. Hiccups are caused when your diaphragm (the wall of muscle between the abdomen and the chest) goes into a spasm, making you breathe in very quickly and causing a cough-like noise as your vocal cords snap shut.

How can you stop hiccups?

There are many ways that are supposed to stop hiccups, such as frightening the victim or putting an ice-cube down his back. The best ways are probably those that steady the breathing, such as drinking water out of the far side of a glass or breathing into a paper (NOT plastic) bag.

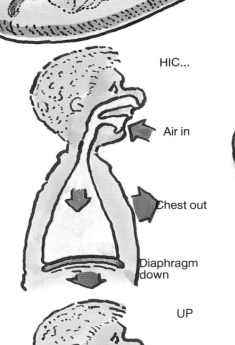

HIC...

Air in

Chest out

Diaphragm down

UP

Air out

Chest in

Diaphragm up

How long does it take to digest a meal?

Food from an average meal spends two to four hours being churned in the stomach before passing into the small intestine. Digestion is completed after a further four to six hours in this 6-metre tube, and the remaining indigestible materials pass into the large intestine. It remains there for up to 15 hours. Within the 1.5 metres of large intestine, water is removed and semi-solid faeces formed.

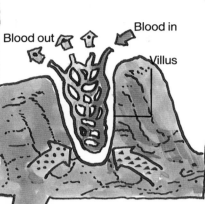

Nutrients are absorbed by small protusions in the small intestine called villi where blood can absorb them

Blood out

Blood in

Villus

Why do we burp?

We burp when gas or wind passes from the stomach through the mouth. The gas may come from drinking fizzy drinks or eating spicy foods. Certain foods, such as cucumber, make many people burp. Burping can also be caused by indigestion. Some people have the habit of swallowing air, which also makes them burp.

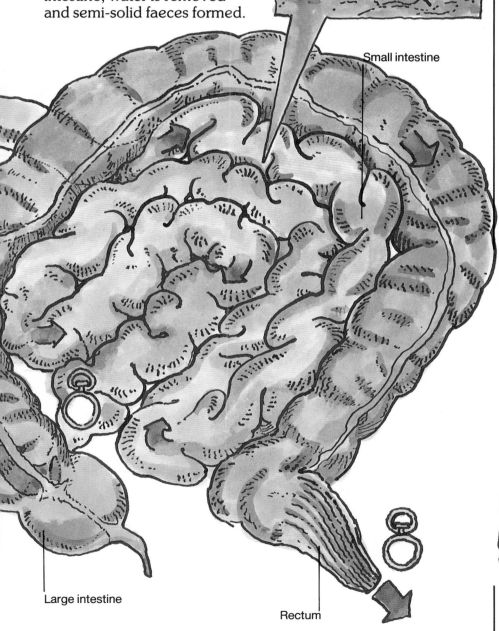

Small intestine

Large intestine

Rectum

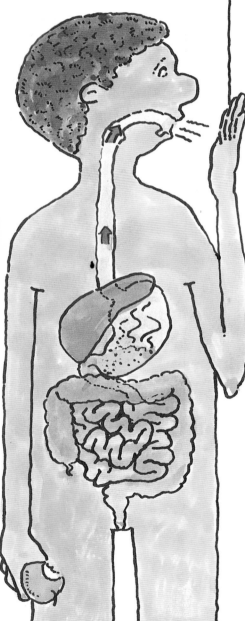

ANSWERS TO QUESTIONS YOU *always* WANTED TO ASK

Why is blood red?

Human blood gets its colour from haemoglobin, which is a complex protein containing iron. Haemoglobin is found in red blood cells, where its job is to carry oxygen from the lungs to the tissues. But not all creatures have red blood. Some animals without backbones, such as insects and spiders, have blue or green blood. This colour comes from a compound of copper, rather than from haemoglobin.

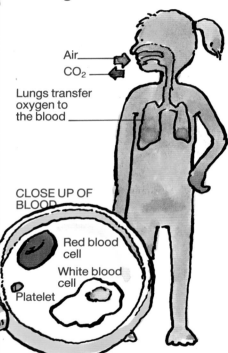

Air

CO_2

Lungs transfer oxygen to the blood

CLOSE UP OF BLOOD

Red blood cell

White blood cell

Platelet

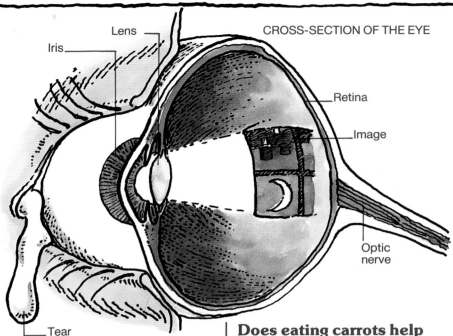

CROSS-SECTION OF THE EYE

Lens

Iris

Retina

Image

Optic nerve

Tear

Why are tears salty?

Tears contain salt, as well as a disinfectant substance that kills germs and so helps prevent the eyes from becoming infected. Tears come from glands just above the eyeballs. Some people have dry eyes because their tear glands do not work properly. They have to use artificial tears from a squeezy bottle.

Does eating carrots help you to see in the dark?

It is a common myth that carrots may help you see in the dark. In reality nobody can see in the pitch black. Good night vision depends on having enough vitamin A which takes part in chemical reactions in the light-sensitive retina at the back of the eyeball. Vitamin A is made in the body from the substance carotene, which occurs in carrots. But too much vitamin A can be poisonous.

Why do we get cramp?

Cramp is a muscle spasm which sometimes occurs after strenuous exercise. The muscle contracts, seizes up and causes an intense pain. It is thought that cramp happens when lactic acid builds up in the muscle. This acid is formed if the blood cannot deliver enough oxygen to keep the muscle working. The cramp usually goes away if the muscle is rested.

Why do we have eyebrows?

Eyebrows act like the dripstones over doors and windows to keep water out of our eyes when it is raining. They also reveal how we feel, rising when we are surprised and knitting together when we are puzzled or angry.

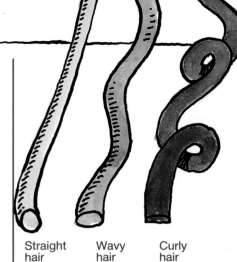

Why do we have finger-nails and toe-nails?

Just like some other mammals – such as apes and monkeys – human beings have nails instead of claws at the ends of their fingers and toes. Our prehistoric ancestors probably used their nails for scratching, grooming and picking their teeth, just as monkeys do today. Nails also back up the fingertips when we hold things. Fingernails grow four times as fast as toenails, which is why they need cutting more often.

Straight hair   Wavy hair   Curly hair

Why do some people have straight hair and some have curly hair?

The straightness of hair depends on the shape of each individual strand. Straight hair is circular in cross-section, like a cylinder. But wavy or curly hair has an oval or flat section. The flatter the hair, the more curly it is.

Why do our ears pop in an aeroplane?

The middle part of the ear and the back of the throat are linked by a narrow tube. Normally the tube keeps the air pressure the same on each side of the ear-drum. But when the cabin pressure in an aeroplane changes rapidly (as it does at take-off and landing), the tube may suddenly become blocked with fluid causing our ears to pop. You can keep the tube open by swallowing.

Why do people get toothache?

Toothache is caused by tooth decay, which occurs when holes form in the teeth. Teeth are made up of a hard substance called dentine covered by a layer of the even harder substance called enamel. Nerves extend into the centre of each tooth. After we eat, small bits of food and bacteria form plaque which sticks to the teeth. Chemicals in the plaque change sugars and starches into lactic acid, which dissolves the enamel and then attacks the dentine. The tooth decays and a hole develops – often exposing the nerve and causing the pain of toothache. A dentist treats the tooth by drilling away the decay and filling the clean hole. You can prevent tooth decay by brushing your teeth regularly and by not eating too much sugary or starchy food.

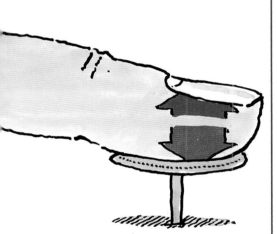

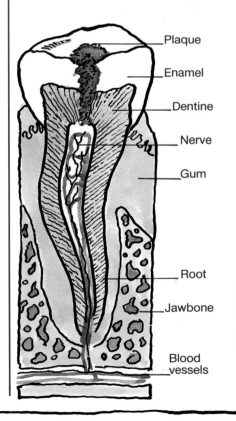

Plaque

Enamel

Dentine

Nerve

Gum

Root

Jawbone

Blood vessels

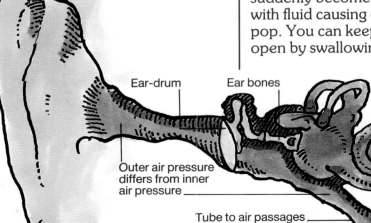

Outer ear

Ear-drum   Ear bones

Outer air pressure differs from inner air pressure

Tube to air passages

Hearing organs

Why are babies born with no teeth?

Babies do have their teeth when they are born, but the teeth are underneath the gums and do not cut through until after six months or so. By the time all the first teeth are through (at about age three) the second teeth are ready and waiting.

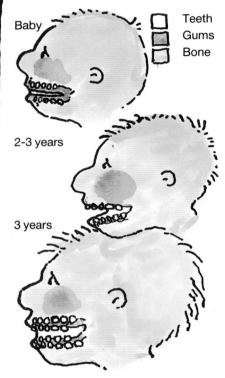

Baby

Teeth
Gums
Bone

2-3 years

3 years

Why do men grow hair on their faces?

Men can grow beards and moustaches because they have male sex hormones. Women and girls do not have male hormones and so do not grow facial hair. Hair starts growing on the face during puberty – it is one of the signs that a boy is becoming a man. Most men trim their beards or shave them off. If a man never shaved, his beard could grow up to 5 metres long!

Why do some men go bald?

Many men begin to lose their hair as they grow older. This is quite normal and often runs in families. Doctors think it may be caused by male sex hormones, which is why women do not go bald in the same way. But men and women can begin to lose their hair for other reasons, such as an illness or because they have to take certain medicines. Nobody has been able to find a cure for natural baldness; some people hide their bald heads under a wig or have a hair transplant.

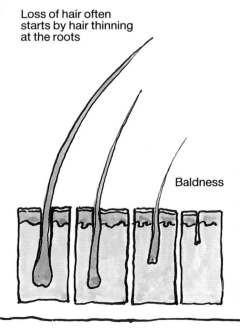

Loss of hair often starts by hair thinning at the roots

Baldness

Why do your hands go wrinkly in the bath?

If you spend a long time in the bath, the water washes away the thin film of natural oil that covers your skin. Without this oil – which comes from tiny glands in the skin – water gets in though tiny pores and makes your skin swell up and wrinkle. After you get out of the bath the skin dries out, and soon shrinks back into shape.

Why do we dream?

Everybody dreams every night, although you probably don't always remember your dreams. Psychiatrists think that things that happen to you in dreams relate in some way to things that have happened in real life. Perhaps dreams help us to sort out memories of previous experiences. When we dream, our eyes move rapidly under our closed eyelids and the electrical activity of our brain speeds up. Nobody knows exactly why we dream, but experiments show that people who are deprived of dream sleep soon become irritable and upset. Then when they are allowed to sleep undisturbed, they have very long dreams.

EVERYDAY THINGS

Why don't birds perching on powerlines get electrocuted?

Birds would only be electrocuted if a large electric current passed through them. For a current to pass through something, some sort of electric circuit has to be made. Birds on a powerline are not touching anything other than the powerline, and so there is nowhere for any current to go to – no circuit is made. If a bird could touch the ground at the same time as the powerline it would be electrocuted instantly.

How do they get the bubbles in fizzy drinks?

The bubbles in fizzy drinks are the gas carbon dioxide. This gas normally dissolves in water only in small amounts. But if the gas is pumped in under pressure, much more dissolves. When you take the top off a bottle the pressure is released, and the gas starts to come out of solution and forms bubbles.

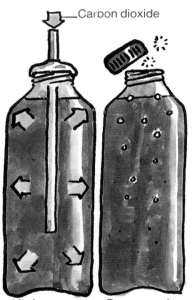

Carbon dioxide

Under pressure   Pressure released

Why don't paper teabags go soggy in water?

Teabags are not made of ordinary paper. Paper is usually made out of wood, cotton, grass and other natural fibres. Teabags are made of a mixture of manila hemp (a very strong natural fibre used for making rope) and plastic fibres. This mixture is resistant to both wetness and heat.

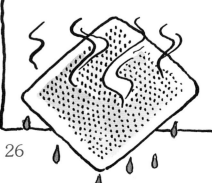

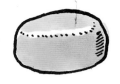

Hard centre

Chocolate added

Heat applied to soften centre but not chocolate

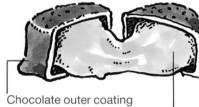

Chocolate outer coating

Soft centre

How do they get the soft centres in chocolates?

First they make hard centres! These are made from sugar and water, and are easy to cover with chocolate. The hard centres contain an enzyme (a substance that causes a chemical reaction to happen). The chocolates are heated to a temperature that makes the enzyme start working (but does not melt the chocolate). The enzyme breaks the sugar down into a form that is more soluble in the water. The sugar partly dissolves and the centre becomes soft.

How do they make instant coffee?

Instant coffee is not made directly from coffee beans, but from prepared coffee. The easiest thing to do is to evaporate all the water from this coffee using hot air. But better quality instant coffee is made by freeze-drying. The coffee is frozen, broken into granules, put into a vacuum chamber and heated gently. Because of the vacuum, the frozen water evaporates directly into water vapour. The low heat and instant evaporation leave more flavour in the coffee.

Coffee made from beans and water

Prepared coffee is frozen

Broken into granules

Gently heated in vacuum

Instant coffee is sealed in a container or jar

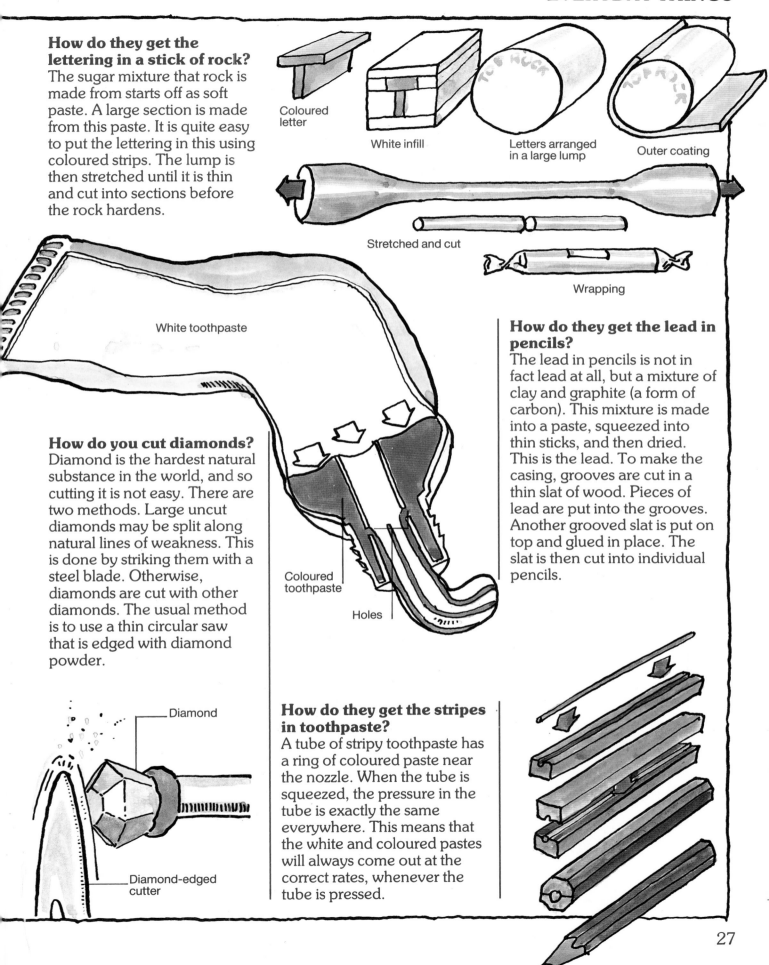

How do they get the lettering in a stick of rock?

The sugar mixture that rock is made from starts off as soft paste. A large section is made from this paste. It is quite easy to put the lettering in this using coloured strips. The lump is then stretched until it is thin and cut into sections before the rock hardens.

Coloured letter

White infill

Letters arranged in a large lump

Outer coating

Stretched and cut

Wrapping

White toothpaste

How do you cut diamonds?

Diamond is the hardest natural substance in the world, and so cutting it is not easy. There are two methods. Large uncut diamonds may be split along natural lines of weakness. This is done by striking them with a steel blade. Otherwise, diamonds are cut with other diamonds. The usual method is to use a thin circular saw that is edged with diamond powder.

Coloured toothpaste

Holes

Diamond

Diamond-edged cutter

How do they get the lead in pencils?

The lead in pencils is not in fact lead at all, but a mixture of clay and graphite (a form of carbon). This mixture is made into a paste, squeezed into thin sticks, and then dried. This is the lead. To make the casing, grooves are cut in a thin slat of wood. Pieces of lead are put into the grooves. Another grooved slat is put on top and glued in place. The slat is then cut into individual pencils.

How do they get the stripes in toothpaste?

A tube of stripy toothpaste has a ring of coloured paste near the nozzle. When the tube is squeezed, the pressure in the tube is exactly the same everywhere. This means that the white and coloured pastes will always come out at the correct rates, whenever the tube is pressed.

How does an aeroplane stay in the air?

As an aeroplane moves through the air – propelled by its engines – air flows over the wings. The wings are more curved on the top than on the bottom. This means that air has to flow more quickly over the top of the wing. Air moving quickly has a lower pressure than air moving slowly. So there is lower pressure above than below the wing. This low pressure sucks up the wing and the aeroplane flies! Ailerons and flaps at the back of the wing and slats at the front are used to increase the curve of the wing for taking off and turning.

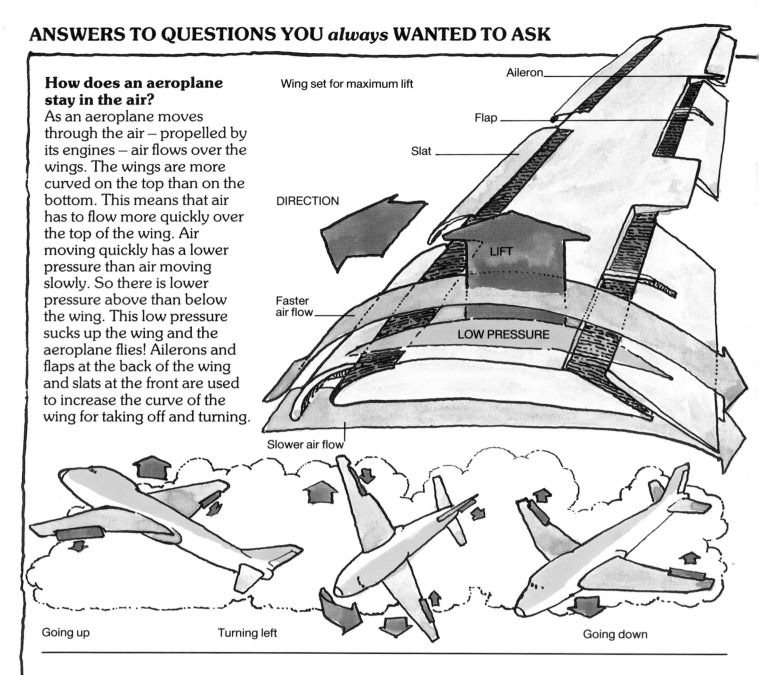

Wing set for maximum lift

Aileron

Flap

Slat

DIRECTION

LIFT

Faster air flow

LOW PRESSURE

Slower air flow

Going up

Turning left

Going down

Front aerofoil

Rear aerofoil

DOWNWARD FORCE

Why do racing cars have wings?

The wings on racing cars are usually known as aerofoils. They have the opposite function to the wings of an aeroplane. Wings lift something up into the air. The aerofoils on a racing car suck the car down onto the ground. This prevents the car from lifting off the road if air gets caught underneath it when it is travelling at a very high speed. It also improves the grip of the car's tyres on the road.

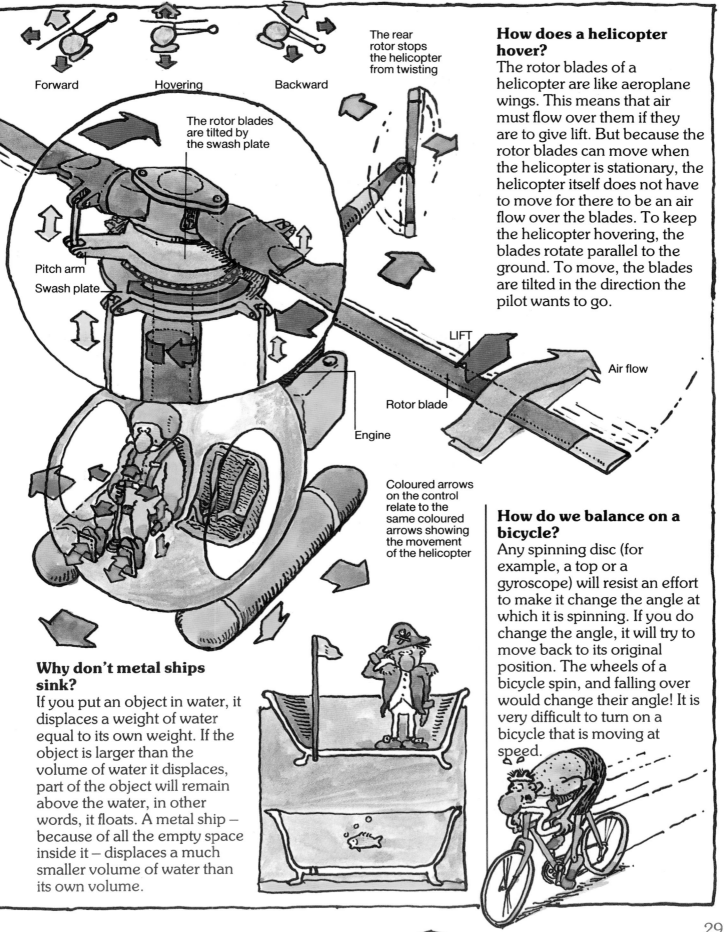

Forward   Hovering   Backward

The rear rotor stops the helicopter from twisting

The rotor blades are tilted by the swash plate

Pitch arm

Swash plate

Engine

Rotor blade

LIFT

Air flow

Coloured arrows on the control relate to the same coloured arrows showing the movement of the helicopter

How does a helicopter hover?

The rotor blades of a helicopter are like aeroplane wings. This means that air must flow over them if they are to give lift. But because the rotor blades can move when the helicopter is stationary, the helicopter itself does not have to move for there to be an air flow over the blades. To keep the helicopter hovering, the blades rotate parallel to the ground. To move, the blades are tilted in the direction the pilot wants to go.

How do we balance on a bicycle?

Any spinning disc (for example, a top or a gyroscope) will resist an effort to make it change the angle at which it is spinning. If you do change the angle, it will try to move back to its original position. The wheels of a bicycle spin, and falling over would change their angle! It is very difficult to turn on a bicycle that is moving at speed.

Why don't metal ships sink?

If you put an object in water, it displaces a weight of water equal to its own weight. If the object is larger than the volume of water it displaces, part of the object will remain above the water, in other words, it floats. A metal ship – because of all the empty space inside it – displaces a much smaller volume of water than its own volume.

How does a vacuum flask work?

A vacuum flask stops heat from travelling either into or out from it. The key to this is a double-walled flask made of silvered glass. Between the walls is a vacuum. Heat can travel in three ways: by radiation (such as the heat we feel from the Sun); by conduction (such as the heat transferred along a poker in a fire); by convection (such as the heating of air from an electric fire). Heat does not radiate in or out because it is reflected by the silvering. It is not conducted in or out because the inside wall of the flask hardly touches the outside wall. And the heat cannot be carried by air because there is no air in the vacuum.

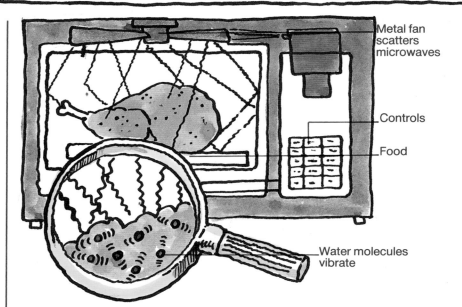

Metal fan scatters microwaves

Controls

Food

Water molecules vibrate

How does a microwave oven cook?

Like any other oven, a microwave oven cooks food by heating it. But it does this in a very different way to a conventional oven. The microwaves (which are similar to radar waves) cause water molecules in the food to vibrate at about 2,500 million times a second. This vibration produces the heat that cooks the food. So dried food without water would not get cooked.

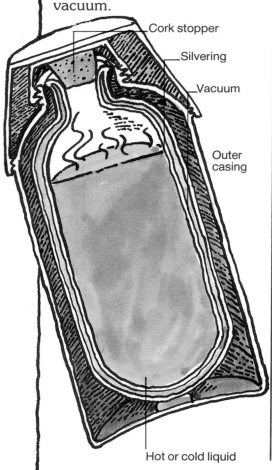

Cork stopper

Silvering

Vacuum

Outer casing

Hot or cold liquid

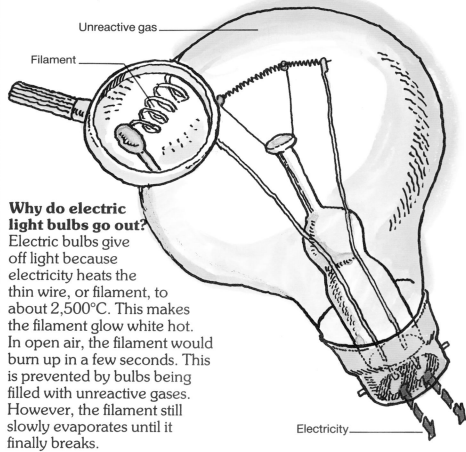

Unreactive gas

Filament

Why do electric light bulbs go out?

Electric bulbs give off light because electricity heats the thin wire, or filament, to about 2,500°C. This makes the filament glow white hot. In open air, the filament would burn up in a few seconds. This is prevented by bulbs being filled with unreactive gases. However, the filament still slowly evaporates until it finally breaks.

Electricity

Why don't plastic handles on cooking pots melt?

There are many types of plastic. A large number, such as thermoplastics, melt at quite low temperatures, but some are very heat resistant, for example, thermosetting plastics such as Bakelite. These thermosetting plastics differ from thermoplastics because they are heated a second time during manufacture. Links form in the polymers (molecular chains) to make a permanent structure. The handles of cooking pots are made of such heat resistant plastics.

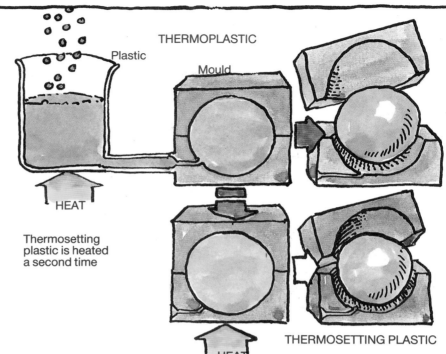

THERMOPLASTIC

Plastic

Mould

HEAT

Thermosetting plastic is heated a second time

HEAT

THERMOSETTING PLASTIC

Where is the vacuum in a vacuum cleaner?

There are two types of vacuum cleaner. In an upright vacuum cleaner, the fan sucks up air and dust, then blows it into the bag. In a canister-type vacuum cleaner, the fan sucks air out of the bag, and so dust and air are pulled into it. In both types of cleaner, the vacuum is only partial and is basically in the place where the fan is. But in a canister-type cleaner, there is also a partial vacuum in the bag.

What makes safety matches safe?

Safety matches will not accidently ignite in the box. They will only light if struck against the striker on the side of the box. This is because they ignite by a chemical reaction between the match head and the striker. Heat generated by friction sets the reaction off.

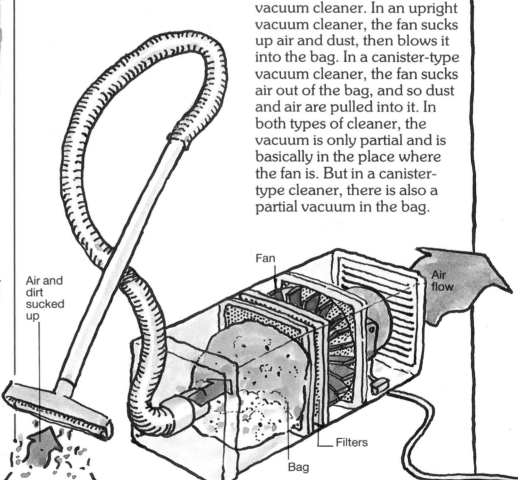

Air and dirt sucked up

Fan

Air flow

Filters

Bag

ANSWERS TO QUESTIONS YOU *always* WANTED TO ASK

Why do floor tiles feel cold?

Floor tiles absorb heat rapidly. This means that if you stand in bare feet on tiles, a lot of heat is drawn out of your foot. A carpet, in comparison, absorbs heat slowly. This means that tiles feel colder than a carpet that is actually the same temperature!

How does a woolly jumper keep you warm?

Air is a poor conductor of heat. But it is good at carrying heat because once it is warmed up it can move rapidly, taking the heat with it. A woolly jumper traps air between its fibres. This air can not move, so the air – being a poor conductor – acts as a good insulator and keeps you warm.

Insulating layer of air

COLD AIR

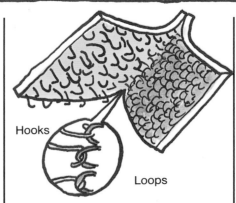

Hooks

Loops

How does Velcro stick?

One part of the Velcro is made of a material covered in hundreds of tiny loops. The other half has hundreds of tiny hooks. So when the two halves are pushed together they stick.

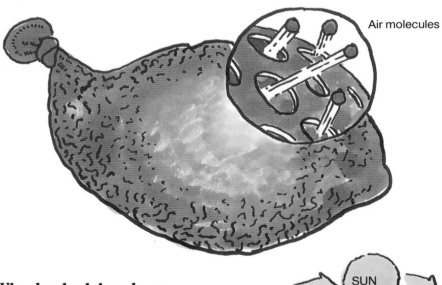

Why do clock hands go round clockwise?

The shadow on sundials turns clockwise (in the Northern Hemisphere). And since long before clocks were made, turning in an anticlockwise direction has been regarded as unlucky. For these two reasons, when people started making clocks they tended to make the hands turn clockwise. Now we are all so used to this that it would be difficult to read clocks if the hands turned the other way.

Why do balloons go wrinkly?

Balloons are made out of rubber. Rubber has an unusual structure, consisting of many long tangled molecules. When a balloon is blown up, the rubber stretches and these molecules straighten out. The rubber becomes slightly porous which allows the air inside to escape very slowly through minute holes. As the balloon deflates, most of the molecules go back to their original position, but some do not and this leaves the balloon wrinkly.

Air molecules

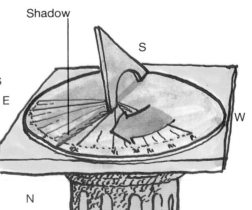

SUN

Shadow

S

E

W

N

Sound waves spread out

Sound waves squashed up

Why does the noise of a police car's siren change as it passes you?

The change of noise is what is known as the Doppler effect. The pitch of a noise depends on how far apart the individual sound waves of a noise are. When a siren is coming towards you, the waves are "squashed" together. When it is moving away from you, the waves are spread out. This means that the pitch of the siren changes as it passes you.

How do building cranes get taller?

The first 10 or so metres of a crane are erected by a mobile crane. After this the building crane erects itself! A new section of tower is hauled up. Hydraulic jacks in the top section raise the cab and the new piece is slotted in and bolted into place.

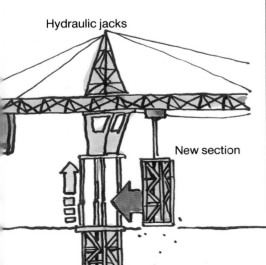

Hydraulic jacks

New section

How do Cat's-eyes shine in the dark?

Cat's-eyes are made from glass tubes held in a metal stud. The back ends of the tubes are reflective, and so the light from car headlights shines back. The studs are held in rubber cases and are pushed down when a car passes over them. This protects them from damage. There are also rubber blades that clean the front of the glass tubes whenever the stud is pressed into its socket.

COLD WEATHER

HOT WEATHER

Why are there gaps in some railway lines?

Metal expands when it is heated. Some metal railway tracks can get several centimetres longer in hot sun. If there were no gaps for the track to expand into, these tracks would bend.

Mirror   Light reflected

LIGHT

Spherical lens

TOP VIEW

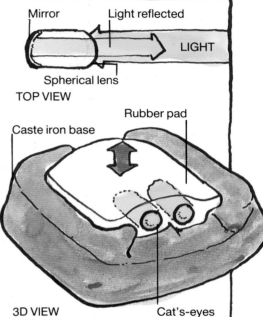

Rubber pad

Caste iron base

3D VIEW   Cat's-eyes

Why do they put salt on the roads in winter?

Adding salt to water lowers the temperature at which it freezes. Salt on roads therefore helps to stop dangerously slippery ice forming.

Why are bubbles round?

Bubbles are a thin film of liquid (usually a mixture of water and a little detergent) filled with air. The air inside the bubble pushes outwards very slightly. The attraction between the water molecules tends to pull the film inwards. The round shape of a bubble is the shape in which these forces are most evenly balanced.

Why do you get a whirlpool when you take out the bath plug?

Amazingly, the whirlpool is caused by the Earth spinning round. This creates forces in the water that deflect it slightly from pouring straight downwards. This effect builds up and a whirlpool starts. In the Northern Hemisphere the water always whirls clockwise; in the Southern Hemisphere it whirls anticlockwise.

Why do portraits look at you when you move?

Portraits do not really look at you, of course. They are only paint! However, the surface of the painted eyeball is flat: a real eyeball is curved. This means that a real eye looks different depending on which way it is looking. The eye in a portrait always looks the same and so, if it is looking outwards, will always seem to be looking at you.

Why do raw onions make you cry?

The strong smell of onions comes from an oil they contain. This oil evaporates easily when an onion is cut or peeled. The vapour from the oil affects nerves in your nose that are connected to your eyes and make your eyes water.

What does the distress call SOS mean?

Before radios were invented messages could be sent by morse code along a telegraph wire. Each letter had a code so abbreviations were often used to shorten the time to make the message. We still use some of those today. One of them is SOS, which means Save Our Souls or Save Our Ship.

What does MAYDAY mean?

MAYDAY is another distress call sent out on the radio to alert anyone who can help. It comes from the French word "M'aidez" which means "Help me".

SPORT AND LEISURE

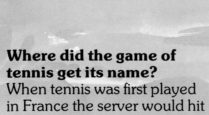

Where did the game of tennis get its name?

When tennis was first played in France the server would hit the ball to his opponent and shout "tenez!" which means "here you are!" in French. The name obviously stuck.

When was soccer invented?

Soccer developed from various games in which two teams tried to move a ball (or some other object) in opposite directions. The earliest known game that resembled football was tsu-chu, which was played in the 4th century BC in China. The Ancient Romans played a similar game. A game rather like football has been played in England since Roman times but was more of a "carrying" game. At Kingston Upon Thames in 1846 a football match between two clubs of unlimited numbers was described in a local paper: "They began at eleven o'clock in the morning and kept the ball until five o'clock in the evening. The rule is to kick the ball throughout the town and whichever club gets the ball nearest the meeting place at five o'clock, wins the game." A proper set of rules for the game we know today was drawn up in England in 1848.

Why do football referees wear black?

It is important that no player mistakes the referee for another player. Most teams play in light or bright colours so that they can be easily distinguished from the other team. So wearing black makes a referee look quite unlike a player.

How do they stitch the last seam on a football?

Footballs are sewn by hand. The pieces are sewn together with the ball inside out. When there is about 15 centimetres of seam unsewn, the ball is turned the right way round. The bladder is inserted and then about 10 centimetres more seam is sewn by reaching into the hole. The last 5 centimetres are stitched very loosely, while the edges of the seam are forced apart. These final stitches are then pulled tight to close the seam.

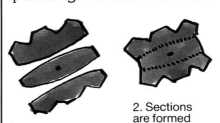

1. Individual segments are stitched together

2. Sections are formed

3. Football stitched inside out

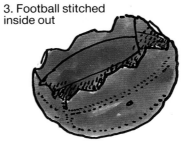

4. Football turned right way round. Bladder is inserted

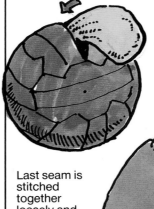

Last seam is stitched together loosely and then pulled tight

Where did the term "try" in rugby originate?

In earlier versions of the game points could only be scored by kicking the ball over the crossbar of the goal. In order to do this a player had to cross his opponents' line with the ball and touch it down. When this happened the crowd would shout "a try, a try" meaning that an attempt to kick at goal could be made. The word gradually became an accepted term for a touchdown with points.

Why are rugby balls the shape they are?

In most ball games, the ball is moved by being struck with a bat, racket, or foot. In rugby and American football, the main way of moving the ball is to carry it and an oval-shaped ball is easier to carry than a round one. It is also more difficult to move it in other ways; for example, it will not easily roll along the ground, and more skill is needed to throw it well.

From where did the term "touchdown" in American football originate?

In modern American football, a team scores when it carries the ball over the other team's goal line. American football developed from rugby, in which the ball must be actually touched down on the ground for a team to score. But in American football the ball does not need to be touched down.

Why is an American football pitch called a gridiron?

A gridiron is a cooking utensil made of parallel metal bars and used for grilling food. An American football pitch has lines marked across it every ten yards, which makes it look something like a very large gridiron.

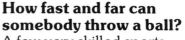

How fast and far can somebody throw a ball?

A few very skilled sports people have been recorded throwing balls (such as cricket balls and baseballs) at just over 160 km/h. And it is not unusual for a good sportsperson to throw at over 130 km/h. The longest recorded throws have been of about 130 metres.

Why are there dimples in golf balls?

The dimples on a golf ball make it travel at least three time further than if it were smooth. If a smooth ball travels through the air, a layer of air sticks to the front surface of the ball. This layer starts to break up and become turbulent further round the ball. The turbulence uses up the ball's energy and slows it down. Dimples make the layer of air stick further round the ball, so there is less drag and the ball has energy to fly further. The dimples also give the ball some lift. When the ball is hit, it spins backwards. The dimples carry air over the top of the ball, and this air travels faster than the air underneath. Faster air has a lower pressure, and so the ball is lifted upwards. The same principle is used to make aeroplanes fly.

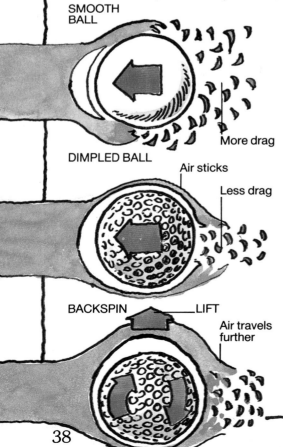

SMOOTH BALL

More drag

DIMPLED BALL

Air sticks

Less drag

BACKSPIN — LIFT

Air travels further

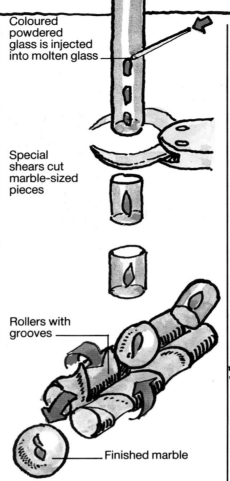

Coloured powdered glass is injected into molten glass

Special shears cut marble-sized pieces

Rollers with grooves

Finished marble

How do they get the coloured bits into marbles?

Molten glass for making marbles is poured out from a large vat in a stream which is about the width of the marble that will be made. Coloured powdered glass is injected into the stream. As the glass falls, it cools and becomes sticky. Special shears cut the glass into marble-sized pieces, and the pieces fall onto a pair of long rollers. The rollers have grooves, rather like those on the bit of a drill. As the rollers turn, the grooves carry the pieces of glass along, rolling them into spheres. The rolling action also puts the twist into the streaks of colour in the marbles.

How do ice skates work?

Ice skates actually slide on water, not ice. When the blade of a skate presses down on ice, the pressure causes a very thin layer of the ice to melt. The skate slides on this thin layer of water. If the ice is too cold, the pressure is not enough to melt the ice, and skates do not work.

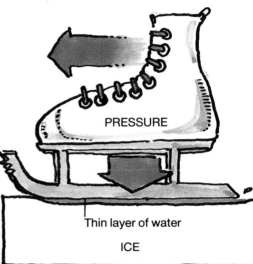

PRESSURE

Thin layer of water

ICE

Why does a bucking bronco buck?

A bucking bronco is an untamed horse. This means that it has not been trained to have a rider on its back. If someone sits on such a horse, it bucks to try to throw the person off.

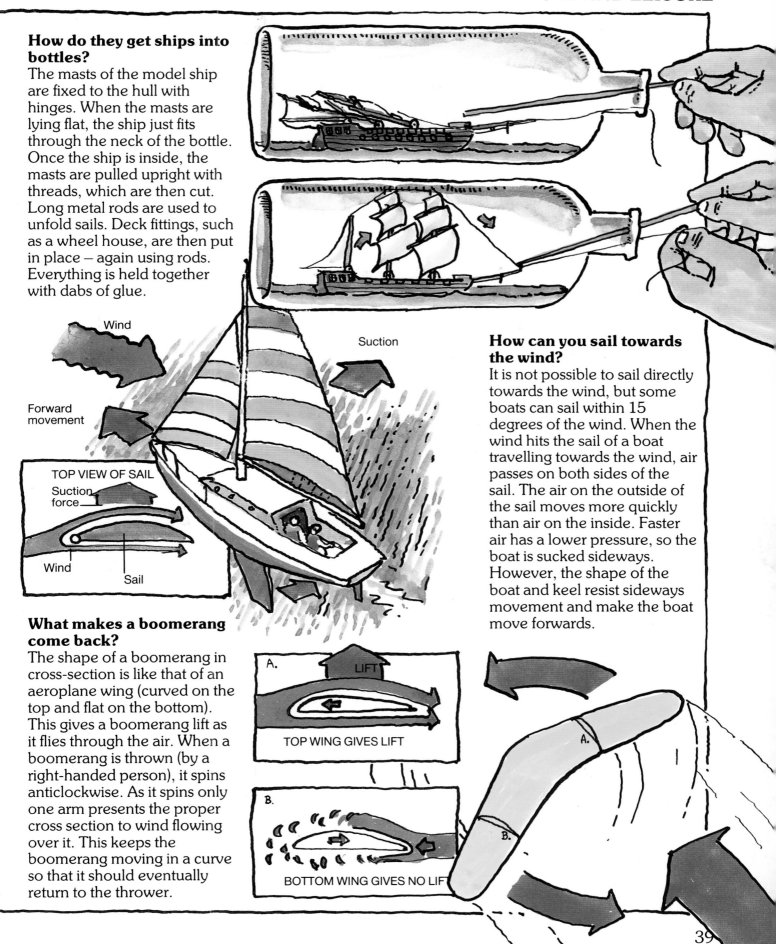

How do they get ships into bottles?

The masts of the model ship are fixed to the hull with hinges. When the masts are lying flat, the ship just fits through the neck of the bottle. Once the ship is inside, the masts are pulled upright with threads, which are then cut. Long metal rods are used to unfold sails. Deck fittings, such as a wheel house, are then put in place – again using rods. Everything is held together with dabs of glue.

Wind

Suction

Forward movement

TOP VIEW OF SAIL

Suction force

Wind

Sail

What makes a boomerang come back?

The shape of a boomerang in cross-section is like that of an aeroplane wing (curved on the top and flat on the bottom). This gives a boomerang lift as it flies through the air. When a boomerang is thrown (by a right-handed person), it spins anticlockwise. As it spins only one arm presents the proper cross section to wind flowing over it. This keeps the boomerang moving in a curve so that it should eventually return to the thrower.

A. LIFT

TOP WING GIVES LIFT

B.

BOTTOM WING GIVES NO LIFT

A.

B.

How can you sail towards the wind?

It is not possible to sail directly towards the wind, but some boats can sail within 15 degrees of the wind. When the wind hits the sail of a boat travelling towards the wind, air passes on both sides of the sail. The air on the outside of the sail moves more quickly than air on the inside. Faster air has a lower pressure, so the boat is sucked sideways. However, the shape of the boat and keel resist sideways movement and make the boat move forwards.

39

ANSWERS TO QUESTIONS YOU *always* WANTED TO ASK

Do professional wrestlers really hurt each other?

Amateur wrestling is a sport of strength and skill. Professional wrestling, however, is more a form of entertainment than a sport. The wrestler's ability to entertain a crowd is often more important than skill at wrestling. But this does not mean that some professional wrestlers are not quite skilful athletes. And they do sometimes really hurt each other in contests, although a lot of the shouting and groaning is just play-acting.

Why does a matador wave a red flag at a bull?

A matador's "flag" is known as a *muleta*. It consists of a piece of cloth hung over a stick. When fighting a bull, the matador uses it to goad the bull into charging. He also uses it to try to guide exactly where the bull charges. Bulls are colour blind, so the red colour of a *muleta* is just a tradition. Matadors also use *capotes*, which are pink.

Do fire-eaters eat fire?

Fire-eaters don't actually eat fire, but they do put the flaming torches into their mouths. The head of the torch is small, and the flame is quickly put out by lack of oxygen. Fire-eaters tilt their heads back so that the heat and flame rise up out of their mouths. The trick is still quite dangerous, however, because the head of the torch remains hot. Fire-eaters also hold petrol in their mouths (but they don't swallow it because petrol is poisonous). They then squirt it out to make jets of flame. This is potentially very dangerous.

Why is the centre of a target called a bull's-eye?

"Bull's-eye" is often used to name things that look like the eye of a bull. Some examples are small thick glass lenses, small round windows, round boiled sweets and the centre of a target.

How fast does a sky diver fall?

Any object falling through air will accelerate until the force of air resistance is equal to the force of gravity. For a falling person, this happens at about 190 km/h. When a sky diver's parachute opens, air resistance increases greatly, and the speed decreases to about 20 km/h.

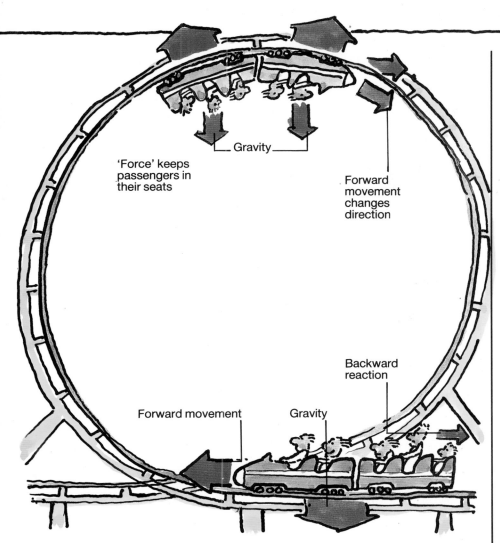

Gravity

'Force' keeps
passengers in
their seats

Forward
movement
changes
direction

Backward
reaction

Forward movement

Gravity

What was the first novel?

It is impossible to say that a particular piece of writing was the first novel. As far back as the Ancient Greeks, there were short pieces of imaginative writing that told a story. However, none of these could be called a novel. For a long time after this, most prose writing told short stories, even if several stories were put together as a group. The first writings that were much like a proper novel appeared in Spain in the 16th and 17th centuries; for example, *Amadis of Gaul* by Garcia Rodriguez de Montevalo in 1508, or *Don Quixote* by Miguel de Cervantes in the early 1600s. The first novel to abandon being a series of stories and instead have one main plot was *Pamela* by Samuel Richardson in 1740.

Why don't you fall out of a roller coaster?

When a roller coaster is upside down as it loops the loop, you are actually held in your seat more strongly than when it is the right way up. Both the roller coaster and you are moving fast. Any moving object will travel in a straight line unless something makes it move in a curve. As the roller coaster changes direction your body wants to continue in a straight line. This "force" keeps you pressed to your seat as the roller coaster continues its change in direction round the loop. The force that keeps you in your seat is greater than the force of gravity, so you don't fall out.

How many possible moves are there in chess?

In the first turn of a game of chess, there are 20 possible moves for each player. After both players have moved, there are 400 possible positions. On the second turn, there are over 50 possible moves for each player. This means that at the end of the second turn there are over a million possible positions. The numbers get rapidly bigger and bigger as a game goes on. In a complete game of chess, there are many billions of possible moves and positions. However, in a particular position, each player rarely has more than a few hundred moves to chose from.

How big was King Kong?

The giant gorilla that crashed across cinema screens in 1933 was about 45 centimetres high! In most scenes with the monster, the model was animated by moving it one frame at a time. Film of the animated model, together with background scenery, was then projected onto a translucent screen from behind (a technique known as back projection). The actors performed in front of the screen.

The model is moved one frame at a time

Real actors are filmed in front of a back projection

How old is Mickey Mouse?

The first Mickey Mouse cartoons appeared in 1928. They were Walt Disney's first big success, and Mickey's voice was spoken by Disney himself. So Mickey Mouse was 60 years old in 1988, and he's still going strong!

How did the Oscars get their name?

The Oscars are officially known as Academy Awards. They were first presented by the Academy of Motion Picture Arts and Sciences in 1928. A golden statuette was designed for presentation to each of the winners. When one of the officials of the Academy first saw the statuette, he remarked that it looked like his uncle Oscar. The name has stuck ever since.

Why do people in old films move so quickly?

People in old films – such as *The Keystone Cops* – did not, of course, actually move more quickly than ordinary people. In fact, it was the camera that moved more slowly. Modern cine cameras take 24 pictures (frames) per second, and modern projectors run at the same speed. Old cameras took 16 to 18 frames per second. This means that if an old film is put into a modern projector it runs too fast. And so everything looks as though it moves too fast. It is possible to slow down some projectors, but television also works at 25 frames a second. You can't slow down everybody's television set! Recently, however, techniques have been developed that can solve this problem.

One second of a cartoon is made from 25 separate drawings

How does Superman fly?

In the Superman film, he usually flies by being held up on a metal arm that is hidden behind him. To make it seem as though he is high up in the air, they use a technique called front projection. A background image is reflected off a two-way mirror in front of the actor. It appears on a screen behind him. The camera films through the mirror. The background image is very faint, so it does not show up on the actor. But the screen is made with glass beads, which intensify the image and make the background bright. You cannot see the shadow of the actor on the screen because he is exactly between the camera and his shadow.

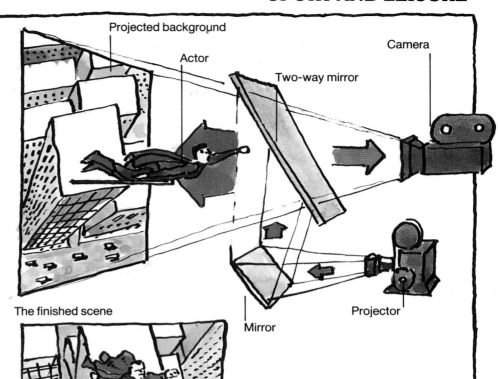

Projected background
Camera
Actor
Two-way mirror
The finished scene
Mirror
Projector

Each individual drawing is photographed separately over a background

Background

Cell overlay with individual drawing

How many drawings are there in a cartoon film?

In a cartoon feature film lasting one and a half hours, there are over 100,000 frames. This means that there are at least 100,000 drawings. In fact, each frame is often made up of several drawings put together. Thus there may be as many as a million drawings in a cartoon feature film. Cheaper cartoons made for television often have many fewer drawings. There may be only a few thousand in a half-hour programme.

ANSWERS TO QUESTIONS YOU *always* WANTED TO ASK

When were the first Olympics?

The first Olympic contest we know about was in 776BC. It took place in the Stadium of Olympia in Greece. There was only one event, a 180 metre foot race, but other events were added in later years. The last ancient Olympics took place in AD394. A modern Olympics was proposed by Baron Pierre de Coubertin. The idea came to him after the ruins of the Stadium at Olympia were discovered in 1875. The first modern games were held in 1896 in Athens.

First Olympic athlete

First modern Olympic athlete

Today's Olympic athlete winning the marathon

What does the Olympic flag mean?

The modern Olympic Games were started mainly to encourage friendship and peace around the world. The five rings represent the continents of Africa, Asia, Australasia, Europe, and North and South America. The rings are joined to symbolize unity among nations. And every nation that competes at the games has at least one of the colours of the flag in its own flag.

Why is the marathon called the marathon?

The marathon race is named after a plain in Ancient Greece that was called Marathon. In 490BC, the Athenians defeated the Persians in a battle at Marathon. Before the battle, the Greek's fastest runner, Pheidippides, went to Sparta (about 250 kilometres away) to fetch help. He then went to Marathon and fought in the battle. Then, so legend has it, Pheidippides ran the 40 kilometres to Athens, shouted, "Rejoice, we conquer", and fell to the ground, dead from exhaustion.

HISTORY

Why do we shake hands?
Shaking hands is a tradition
that has grown up over
hundreds if not thousands of
years. It probably originated in
order to show that you did not
have anything concealed in
your hand, such as a weapon.
So it started as a sign of trust.

ANSWERS TO QUESTIONS YOU *always* WANTED TO ASK

What is prehistory?
People first started to write about 5,500 years ago. Time before this is known as prehistory. So prehistory is not the time before history (if there could be such a time!), but the time before there was any written history.

FALL OF ROME (AD400-500)

MIDDLE AGES

ITALIAN RENAISSANCE (BEGAN AD1400s)

What were the Stone, Bronze and Iron ages?
Archaeologists use these terms to classify early periods of human history. The terms refer to the main material used to make tools in the periods. The materials reflect the development of culture at the time. The Stone Age began about 2 million years ago and lasted until the Bronze Age, which started about 3,000BC. The Iron Age began between 1,500 and 1,000BC.

What were the Middle Ages in the middle of?
The Middle Ages were the period in Europe between the end of ancient times and beginning of modern times. Historians generally consider the end of ancient times to be the fall of the Roman Empire between AD400 and AD500. The beginning of modern times is regarded as the start of the Italian Renaissance, the great flourishing of arts and sciences in the 1400s.

Why were the Dark Ages dark?
The period in the history of Europe known as the Dark Ages lasted roughly from AD500 to AD1000 (the first half of the Middle Ages). The word "dark" refers to a lack of learning and knowledge during this time. Many of the technical and artistic skills from the ancient civilizations were lost, as was much other knowledge. Modern historians, however, have realized that the Dark Ages were not as dark and dreary as everyone used to think they were.

Stone Age arrow head

Bronze Age spear head

Iron Age dagger

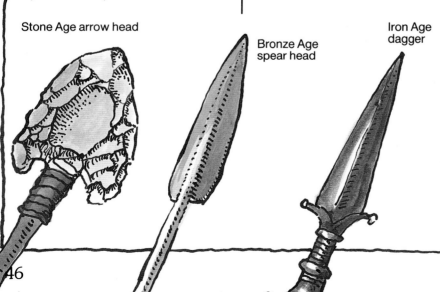

Where did the first people come from?

It is difficult to say who the first humans really were. There were originally a number of human-like species. Most scientists regard *Homo habilis* as the first true group of humans. They lived in Africa about two million years ago, and used stone tools. Fossils have been discovered in Kenya and other parts of East Africa.

AFRICA

Kenya

Did cavemen live in caves?

A few of them did. Most Stone Age people lived in shelters built from branches, animal hides and other natural materials. There simply would not have been enough caves to go round for all of them! However, caves do not fall down easily, so they are the only "cavemen" houses we can still see.

When was money first used?

Before money was used, people would always barter goods. As time went by, certain goods (such as shells or metals) became standard items that everyone would accept in exchange. Coins were first made as a convenient form of precious metal with a known weight, and so a known value. The earliest coin discovered was made between 600 and 700BC in Lydia (now part of western Turkey).

Where did the dollar and pound signs come from?

The dollar sign is a stylized figure 8. This originates from the old Spanish coin called a piece of eight, which was worth eight reals. The pound sign is a stylized letter L. This originates from the Ancient Roman coin, the librum. The sign is also sometimes used for Italian lira.

Piece of eight

$

Roman Librum

£

How did people pay taxes before money was invented?

People paid with goods. For example, a farmer might pay taxes to a local landowner with a part of the harvest from his land. A common tax was known as a tithe; this was a tenth of what a person had produced a year.

ANSWERS TO QUESTIONS YOU *always* WANTED TO ASK

Who invented the wheel?

The wheel was probably invented between 5,000 and 6,000 years ago in Mesopotamia (part of what is now Iraq). The wheel developed from using rollers to move heavy objects, such as massive stones for building. A wheel is essentially a slice through a very large roller. The first wheels would probably have been solid disks of wood, made of planks clamped together.

Why did the Aborigines invent the boomerang?

The Australian Aborigines used boomerangs as hunting weapons. There are two types of boomerang: returning and non-returning. The Aborigines mainly used the non-returning type. The advantage of a boomerang is that it spins, and so hits its target with more force than, for example, a thrown rock. Returning boomerangs are not good for most hunting because their curved flight-path makes them difficult to aim. Their advantage, however is that you do not have to go a long way to get it back and they do not get lost so easily.

Who were the first people to drink beer?

Beer was not the first alcoholic drink to be made, but it has been drunk since at least 6,000 years ago. The ancient Babylonians and Assyrians had beer, and archaeologists have discovered an Ancient Egyptian brewery!

Why did the Egyptians build pyramids?

Pyramids were built as enormous tombs for kings and queens. The Egyptians believed in an afterlife. They also believed that surviving in the afterlife depended on the continued existence of the physical body. They also thought that a supply of the things needed for earthly existence was necessary. The pyramids protected the king's or queen's body and their supplies. They were also monuments to the power and wealth of the ruler.

Why did the Romans build their roads in straight lines?

The main reason for this is that the shortest distance between two places is a straight line. It is therefore a sensible way to build roads if you can do it. The Romans had developed the surveying and road-building techniques that were necessary for building straight roads.

Why are destructive people called vandals?

The word vandal comes from the Vandals, who were a tribe of barbarians from northern Europe. They invaded much of southern Europe, sacking Rome in AD455. They were often very destructive in the territory they invaded, although not necessarily very much worse than many other barbarian tribes.

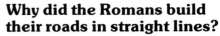

Chain mail

Metal plate

Were there really knights in shining armour?

Knights were a social class in the Middle Ages who owned land and fought in times of war. Until the 1300s, the armour knights wore was made of linked chains, which would hardly shine at all. Patches of metal plate (which can shine) then started to be used, until in the 1400s a knight was completely covered in plate armour. But in reality, this armour was not polished very brightly. Knights were supposed to have a code of conduct, which included helping the weak and poor. But they often did not live up to their chivalric aims.

Why are American Indians called Indians?

The answer to this question is that it was a mistake! When Columbus crossed the Atlantic and discovered America, he was looking for a route to the Indies (which then consisted of India and eastern Asia). When he arrived in America he thought he had arrived in the Indies, and so called the inhabitants Indians.

Why did they stop building castles?

Castles were built to defend the people inside them. For a long time it was very difficult for an attacker to get in; usually the only method was a long siege. When gunpowder and canons were invented, it started to become quite easy to knock holes in the wall of a castle – and a castle was a very big target! People quite quickly stopped building them.

How did countries get their names?

Much the most common reason for a country's name is the main group of people who lived there at some time in its history. For example, England comes from Angle land, and France is named after the Franks. Sometimes there are special reasons, such as with America. America is named after Amerigo Vespucci, who claimed to have been the first person to sail to America and realize that it was a new continent (Columbus did not realize this)!

How did they discover that the world was round?

Through the Middle Ages, almost everyone thought the world was flat. But by the 1400s, many people started to think that it was a sphere. There was no proof, however, until someone had reached a known part of the world by sailing westwards. The first person to do this was Ferdinand Magellan. In AD1519, he sailed from Spain, rounded the southern tip of South America and reached the East Indies.

Ferdinand Magellan

49

ANSWERS TO QUESTIONS YOU *always* WANTED TO ASK

Why does Genghis Khan have such a terrible reputation?

Genghis Khan and his armies conquered large parts of central Asia in the late twelfth and early thirteenth centuries. They seemed invincible and caused great destruction and bloodshed wherever they conquered. They often killed any prisoners they took, and used terror wherever they went. To his credit, Genghis Khan promoted law, order and literacy among his own people.

Why was Alexander the Great so great?

Alexander was king of Macedonia, part of Ancient Greece, over 300 years before Christ. He was a great general, conquering an empire that included Egypt and stretched as far as the west of India. But he also spread Greek culture and learning to all the areas he conquered. Greek culture was the most advanced of its time.

Was there really a Count Dracula?

Count Dracula was a character made up by Bram Stoker in his Victorian novel about vampires. However, the novel was based on old vampire legends about Vlad Tepes, a prince in Transylvania in the 1400s. He was known as Vlad the Impaler, and committed hundreds of murders to suppress the local population.

Did Drake really finish his game of bowls when the Armada attacked?

It is possibly true that Drake was playing bowls when he heard that the Spanish Armada was approaching England. It may even be true that he finished the game before going to his ship. The Armada was still too far away to attack, and his fleet was well prepared. However, the story is probably a legend to show how courageous the great hero was!

Vlad Tepes

MACEDONIA

BACTRIA

PERSIA

PARTHIA

EGYPT

Alexander the Great

Francis Drake

Genghis Khan

How did Ivan the Terrible get his name?

Ivan the Terrible came to the throne of Russia in 1547. He was ruthless and cruel. He set up fierce laws and enforced them with executions and terror. For example, he suspected the Russian town of Novogorod of planning to join with Poland, so he sacked it, killing 60,000 people. Another of his deeds was to kill his eldest son with his own hands. He was first called "the Terrible", however, after a series of battles in which he defeated Mongol invaders.

Ivan the Terrible

Why did Nelson ask Hardy to kiss him?

Nobody really knows, because Nelson died shortly afterwards so could never explain! However, many people think that he did not actually say "kiss me", but "kismet". Kismet means fate or destiny, and so Nelson would have been saying that he accepted his fate of dying in battle.

Why is Napoleon sometimes shown holding his stomach?

Napoleon was a powerful emperor, so would have been able to choose exactly how he was shown in portraits. He probably thought that putting his hand inside his waistcoat looked elegant! He did walk around with his hand on his stomach a lot of the time anyway, because he suffered from bad indigestion.

Napoleon Bonaparte

Why was Churchill always sticking two fingers in the air?

Churchill didn't always have two fingers in the air. But he was often photographed that way during World War II. The two fingers formed a V, which was a sign for victory.

Why does Father Christmas come down the chimney?

The legend of Father Christmas started with St Nicholas, who lived in the AD 300s. He was known for taking presents to the poor. Some ancient houses (or huts) only had one entrance: a hole in the roof, which let smoke from the fire out and let people in down a ladder. So the only way to enter a house was down the "chimney".

Churchill

Nelson

51

ANSWERS TO QUESTIONS YOU *always* WANTED TO ASK

Who was responsible for the habit of smoking?

The first people known to smoke were American Indians. They did not all smoke tobacco. For example, some North American Indians smoked red willow bark. Tobacco (and so the habit of smoking) was brought to Europe from South America by several people. For example: Sir Walter Raleigh brought it to Britain; Jean Nicot (after whom nicotine is named) introduced it to France; Peter Stuyvesant took it to the Netherlands.

Did they drink tea at the Boston Tea Party?

The Boston Tea Party was not in fact a party at all. It was a raid by American colonists in 1773 on a number of British ships moored in Boston harbour. They were objecting to a tax the British goverment had put on tea. The ships were loaded with tea, and the colonists tipped it all into the harbour. Any tea drinking was done by fish!

What turned round in the Industrial Revolution?

The Industrial Revolution was a time of enormous technical innovation, particularly in manufacturing industry. So one answer to the question might be the wheels of a large number of newly invented machines! But this is not what is meant by the "Revolution". It refers to the enormous changes that took place, "turning round" the lives of people, the economics and history of the world, and the development of science.

One of the major technical innovations of the Industrial Revolution was the steam engine

NATURE

How does a chameleon change colour?

Stories of a chameleon's ability to change colour are often exaggerated. They cannot change to any colour at all (for example, a chameleon could not become bright red), but they can still make quite dramatic changes. Underneath a chameleon's skin are three types of colour-containing cells: red, yellow and brown. These can change in size, and so alter the colour of the skin. There is a reflecting layer under the cells that helps to blend the colours. Chameleons change colour both to camouflage themselves and to show their moods.

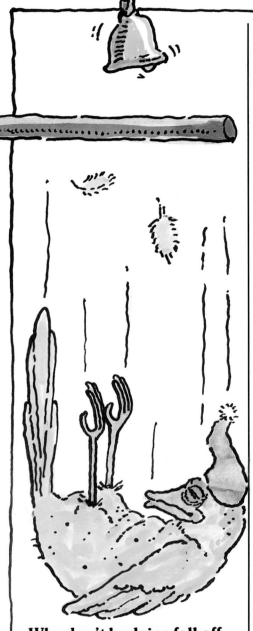

How do earthworms move?

An earthworm is divided into many segments. Each segment can get longer and thinner or shorter and thicker. Waves of lengthening and shortening pass down the worm's body. When a section lengthens, it pushes the head forwards. As it contracts, it pulls the back of the worm forwards. Thicker contracted segments anchor parts of the worm that are not moving to the ground. Movement is helped by small bristles called *chaetae* on the underside of the worm. They point backwards. This makes it easier for the body to slide forwards than backwards. Earthworms move in the same way when they are burrowing.

Why don't budgies fall off their perches when asleep?

Birds like budgerigars spend a lot of their time perching on branches and twigs. Their feet have evolved so that when clinging to branches the muscles and tendons of the feet are at rest. If you see a dead bird you will notice its toes are curled up. Therefore when they sleep they naturally grip the perch. Automatic reflexes keep the bird from toppling over without waking it up.

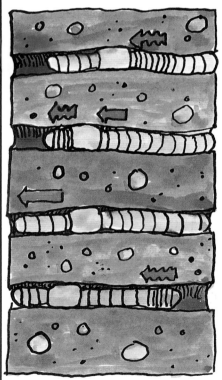

Earthworm

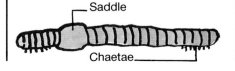
Saddle

Chaetae

Why do fish swim in shoals?

Fish swim in shoals to protect themselves from predators. A predator is more likely to be seen, because a shoal has many pairs of eyes. When a predator attacks, it may be confused by the large numbers of fish. And the chances of any individual being attacked are reduced. About one in five species of fish regularly live in shoals. But many other fish also come together in large groups for spawning. Swimming in a shoal also provides a more streamlined way of moving through water.

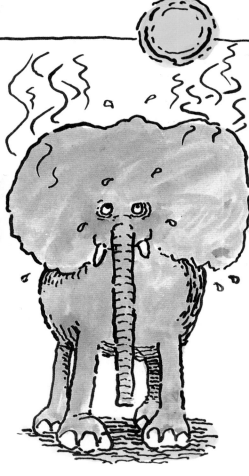

Why do wolves howl at the moon?

It is doubtful that wolves really do howl at the moon. The reason for the legend is probably that you can only see wolves howling on moonlit nights. Wolves point their noses to the sky when howling even if there is no moon at all. Nobody knows for sure why wolves howl, but it could be a form of communication.

Why do elephants have such big ears?

The enormous body of an elephant means that there is always a danger it will over-heat in the hot sun. Elephants use their ears to keep cool, rather like a car radiator. As the warm blood flows around the large surface area of the ears a breeze will cool it down. Elephants help this process by flapping their ears in the air.

Do hyenas really laugh?

Hyenas do not laugh. They simply have a sort of howl that sounds a bit like human laughter. Perhaps they would not have much to laugh about if they could. Hyenas have a bad reputation as unpleasant scavengers, which is very unfair. They do scavenge for food, but they are also efficient and skilful hunters.

Why do giraffes have such long necks?

Giraffes live in parts of the world where food can be very scarce, particularly at dry times of year. There can be a lot of competition among grazing animals for the little food that there is. To deal with this, giraffes use their long necks and legs. This means that they can eat leaves that other animals cannot reach.

How do we know what dinosaurs looked like?

From fossil records! Sometimes when a dinosaur died its remains were covered by mud or sand. Over thousands of years the layers of mud or sand piled up and turned to rock under pressure. Chemicals in the rock seeped into the remains and eventually turned them into rock too. Usually only hard parts like bones and shells become fossils, as soft parts like flesh and internal organs rot too quickly. Footprints and eggs can also be fossilized. When fossils are discovered they are carefully excavated and reassembled to form skeletons. From this experts can work out how muscles and other organs might have fitted to produce a model of how the dinosaur might have looked.

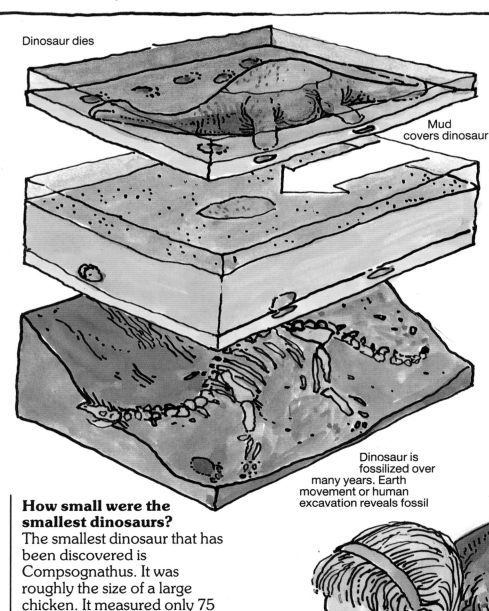

Dinosaur dies

Mud covers dinosaur

Dinosaur is fossilized over many years. Earth movement or human excavation reveals fossil

How were baby dinosaurs born?

Dinosaurs were a sort of early reptile. Like modern reptiles, such as crocodiles, they laid eggs. The eggs varied in size depending on the size of the dinosaur, but the largest was over 30 centimetres long.

Dinosaur hatching from egg

How small were the smallest dinosaurs?

The smallest dinosaur that has been discovered is Compsognathus. It was roughly the size of a large chicken. It measured only 75 centimetres from nose to tail, and weighed about 6.8 kilograms.

Compsognathus

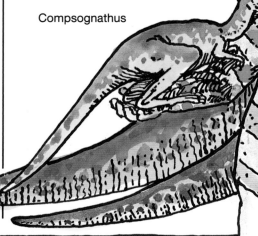

How big were the largest dinosaurs?

It is difficult to be sure what kind was the largest dinosaur. There may be many that have never been discovered. Also, the whole skeleton of a dinosaur is not always found, and so guesswork must be used. The tallest and heaviest dinosaur for which there is a whole skeleton was a Brachiosaurus, which was 6 metres high at the shoulder, and probably weighed 35-50 tonnes. However, such dinosaurs as Ultrasaurus may have been 30 metres long and weighed 130 tonnes.

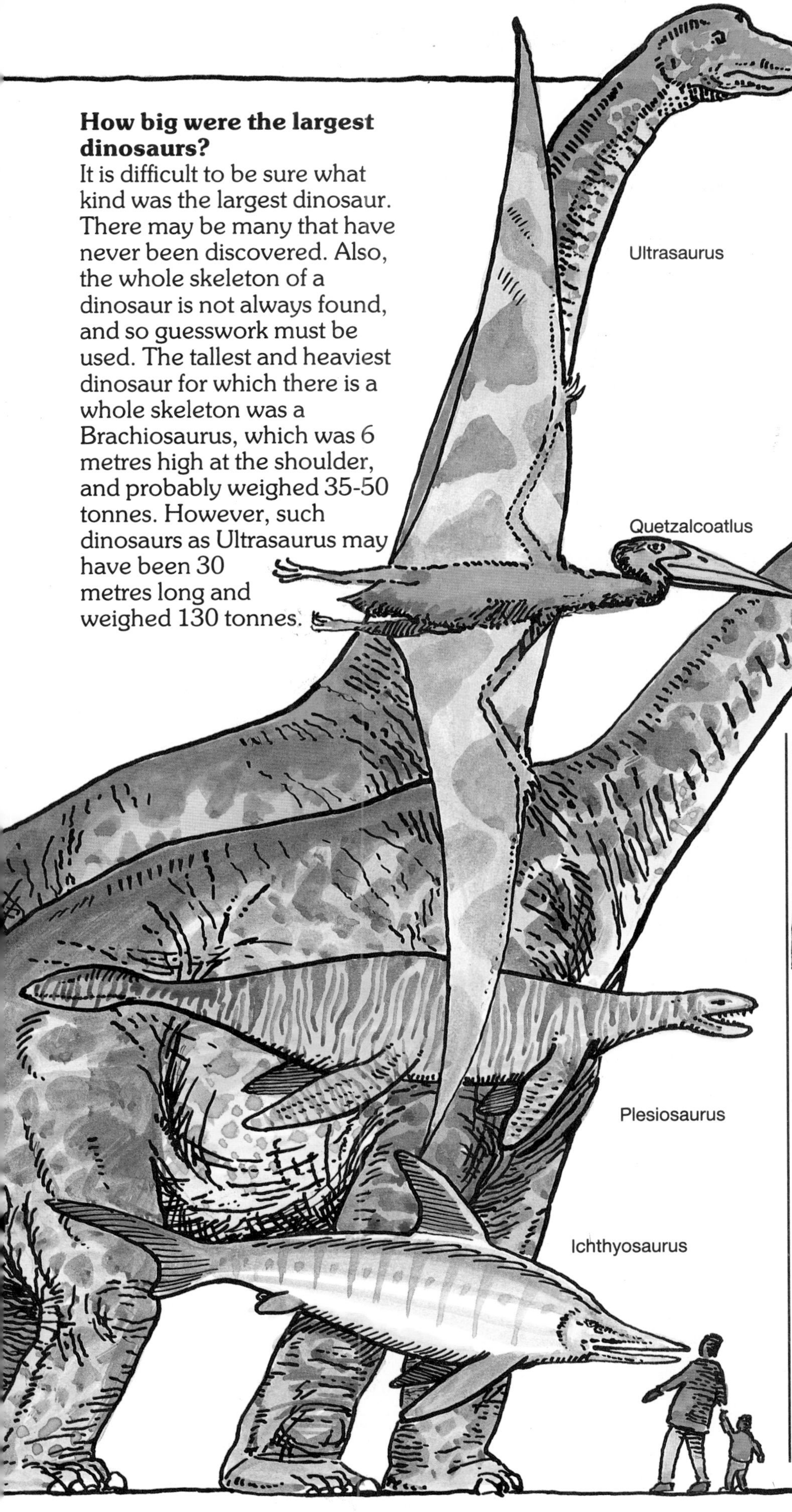

Ultrasaurus

Quetzalcoatlus

Plesiosaurus

Ichthyosaurus

Could any dinosaurs fly or swim?

There were large flying and swimming reptiles at the time of the dinosaurs, but these are not usually thought of as dinosaurs. An example of a flying reptile is the enormous Quetzalcoatlus northropi, a pterosaur. It had a wingspan of as much as 12 metres. There were many swimming reptiles, including plesiosaurs and ichthyosaurs.

Brachiosaurus

What happened to the dinosaurs?

Nobody is quite sure why the dinosaurs died out. There have been many theories. The most common is that about 65 million years ago the Earth's climate cooled down quite rapidly. Vegetation changed, so there was little food for plant eaters; and as they died out, there was little food for meat eaters. Long periods of cold weather could have killed dinosaurs directly. They had no fur to protect them and were too large to hide in burrows.

57

ANSWERS TO QUESTIONS YOU *always* WANTED TO ASK

Jaw bones dislocate themselves when swallowing huge objects

Egg-eating snake

How does a snake swallow something bigger than its head?

Some snakes, such as pythons and egg-eating snakes, can swallow things that are many times bigger than their heads. For example, a large python with a head less than 30 centimetres across can swallow an antelope with a body over a metre wide. The main secret to this is that their jaws can dislocate themselves and come apart. Also, the skin at the side of the mouth can stretch enormously. This means that the snake can make its mouth, and so its head, many times larger.

Do cows ever run out of milk?

A cow can carry on producing milk for most of its life. But only as long as it is milked regularly. When a cow has a calf, it starts to produce milk. It will continue to provide milk as long as the calf needs it. A cow's udders, therefore, produce milk for as long as it is taken from them. But illness or a bad shock can stop a cow producing milk. A milking cow normally has a calf each year.

How do homing pigeons find their way home?

Some scientists think that pigeons have an ability to detect the Earth's magnetic field. This would mean that they could fly using a sort of "compass" in their brain. Other people think that they fly using the position of the Sun to find their way. There is no definite evidence for either of these theories. In what ever way they do it, pigeons have been know to fly more than 2,000 kilometres over unknown country to get home.

Do fish sleep?

When fish sleep, their bodies slow down, but their brain wave patterns don't change. They have no eyelids so they can't close their eyes, but they do become rather less aware of their surroundings. So fish do sleep, but not quite in the way that most mammals do.

Why do I find spiders in the bathtub?

The main reason is that they get stuck there. There are more spiders than you realize walking around in houses. Once a spider has walked into a bathtub, the sides are too slippery for it to climb out again. The bathtub acts like a kind of spider trap.

Why do cats purr?

Like all animal noises, a cat's purr is a form of communication. It shows pleasure, comfort and friendship. Cats are unusual because they have two sets of vocal cords, one above the other. Many scientists think that they use the lower set for meows and high-pitched noises, and the higher set for growls, purring and low-pitched noises.

Why don't fish living in the Arctic Sea freeze?

The temperature of the water in the Arctic sea can be below the normal freezing temperature of water. This is because salt reduces the freezing point. Most fish do not have nearly as much salt in them as there is in the sea, so there is a real risk of the fish freezing. To avoid this, they have special substances (glycoproteins) in their bodies. These substances work just like the antifreeze you put in car radiators in winter.

Why do zebras have black and white stripes?

The stripes are for camouflage. This may seem surprising, because the stripes seem to make zebras very visible. But the stripes break up the outline of a zebra. At a distance, anything with a broken outline is more difficult to see. Stripes also help if a herd of zebras is being attacked. Many striped zebras all running together can confuse the attacker. Battleships in the First World War adopted this type of camouflage by having large striped patterns in black and white painted on them to prevent the enemy finding the correct range.

Why do bats hang upside down?

Many species of bat roost in caves. They also live in other dark sheltered places. It is much safer for bats to roost off the ground if they can. In caves, however, there is not much to hold on to except the roof. This means that bats have to hang upside down. Bats that live in caves have specially adapted claws to hold on to hard rock surfaces.

59

Why are most plants green?

Plants make much of their food by a process called photosynthesis. This involves absorbing sunlight and using the energy to manufacture its food. The light is absorbed by a special pigment called chlorophyll, which is usually green. A few plants, such as red seaweed, use chlorophyll which is a different colour.

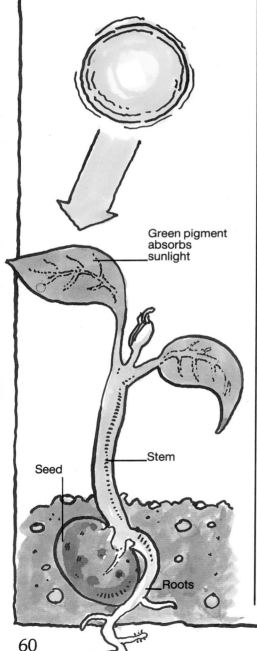

Green pigment absorbs sunlight

Stem

Seed

Roots

Why are some plants carnivorous?

Carnivorous plants like the sundew, butterwort, pitcher plant, and Venus flytrap live in marshes and bogs. The soil in such places is lacking in nutrients, especially nitrogen. Nitrogen is very important for making proteins and similar substances. To make up for the poor soil, these plants catch and digest insects. Insects contain plenty of nitrogen (because they contain a lot of protein), as well as other minerals.

How do seedless grapes reproduce?

Seedless grapes have no seeds to produce new plants. They can only reproduce by human intervention. Cuttings are taken from a seedless grape vine and grafted onto the stem of another sort of grape. This is, in fact, how most grape varieties are reproduced by farmers.

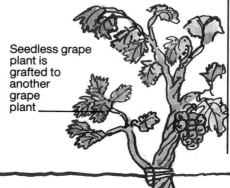

Seedless grape plant is grafted to another grape plant

Why does a Mexican bean jump?

A Mexican bean (also called a jumping bean) does not move on its own. Inside the bean is a caterpillar. A moth lays an egg in the bean and the caterpillar hatches out. The caterpillar feeds off the inside of the bean. Its movement makes the bean move. Mexican beans usually roll around more than they really jump.

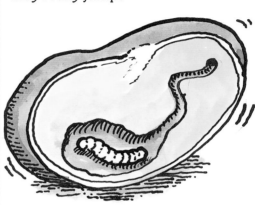

Why do cactuses have so many thorns?

Cactuses live in areas of the world where there is very little water. They deal with this problem by storing a lot of water inside them. Animals living in the same areas also have a problem with getting enough water. A juicy cactus is a tempting snack to them, because it holds a lot of water. Cactuses are quite soft, so they need thorns to stop themselves being eaten.

Why do trees lose their leaves in winter?

In the summer, trees are always drawing water out of the ground, and as they do so they evaporate water from their leaves. As the water evaporates, more water is pulled into the leaves from tubes in the branches and trunk. These in turn pull water up from the roots. In winter, the water in the ground is often frozen, and so trees can not draw it into their roots. If a tree did not lose its leaves, it might lose too much of its water and die. Some trees in hot climates lose their leaves in the summer to save water.

SUMMER

Water evaporates from leaves

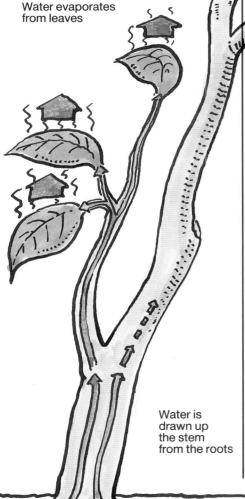

Water is drawn up the stem from the roots

WINTER

Leaves fall off

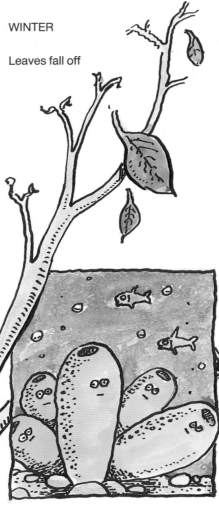

Is a sponge an animal or a plant?

People used to think that sponges were plants. Like a sort of seaweed, they live attached to the sea bed and never move. Sponges are, however, animals. They can have quite complex shapes, but internally are very simple. There are no special organs, and they have nothing like a head or a nervous system. In many ways, each sponge is more like a colony of tiny individual animals. If you break up a sponge into individual cells (by putting it through a fine sieve), the cells will join together to form a new sponge.

What is the oldest living thing on Earth?

Trees live much longer than any other type of plant or animal. It is possible to know the age of a tree by counting the rings in its trunk. One ring grows each year. The oldest living tree, and so the oldest known living thing, is a bristlecone pine in California. It is over 4,600 years old.

Bristlecone pine

61

INDEX

PRINTED IN BELGIUM BY proost INTERNATIONAL BOOK PRODUCTION